Christmas 1985

D1124310

Copies of

PROVEN PERFORMANCES

may be obtained from:

Bobbee Ferrer
3321 Ridgeway Drive
Metairie, Louisiana 70002

Copyright 1985
Library of Congress Catalog Card Number: 85–51914
ISBN 0-9615869-0-7

Cover Drawing by: Jon Russo
Section Covers illustrated by:
Virginia Neary
and
Howard Battle

Printed in the U.S.A.
WIMMER BROTHERS, INC.

FOREWARD
By Ron Virgets

Be forewarned: This foreward is a first.

But there are several reasons why this is a good place for me to start.

The origins of this project sprang from the wish of Bobbee Ferrer to become more familiar with the world of horseracing, the world of her jockey agent-husband Joe. It's a world of complexities and warmth, but a world that can be extraordinarily difficult for the newcomer to penetrate.

So Bobbee Ferrer set out to meet the people of that world and we're all the better for her quest. Because she has brought us in contact with those people, big names and small, in a new and very warm and human way.

Everyone from chorus girls to chemistry professors has cookbooks out there now, but I can think of two ready facts that are going to make this a very special cookbook.

First, the nomadic nature of their work exposes racetrackers to a wide variety of cuisines and if, say, you want an educated comparison of Louisiana and Maryland seafood, talk to the horseman who winters at the Fair Grounds and summers at Pimlico.

Second, again by the nature of their work, racetrackers are attuned to the basics of this life. Its' joys and trials and the short distances between them are part of their inner fabric and so are some of life's more uplifting sights and sounds. And tastes.

And oh, what tastes. While she was putting this book together, Bobbee was kind enough to invite me over to try out many of the recipes, platonic dishes like Vincent Timphony's Barbecued Shrimp, Randy Romero's Redfish Sauce Picquant, Futurity Fudge Pie, Homemade Linguini with white clam sauce....

Let me not detain you any longer. Turn the page and let Bobbee Ferrer introduce you to some of the most provocative recipes offered anywhere and reintroduce you to some old racing names, seen in a new light.....

Acknowledgements

I am pleased to present to you a collection of recipes by and for Thoroughbred racing enthusiasts. This very special cookbook contains regional flavors from all over the country contributed by leaders in the Thoroughbred racing industry. My sincere thanks to all who helped to create PROVEN PERFORMANCES by submitting their favorite recipes.

My family and friends deserve credit for their willing participation in recipe testing and tasting, the latter expressed as the most enjoyable of the two. We may have gained a few unwanted pounds in the process, but what a wonderful time we enjoyed together.

A final word of thanks to my husband who has been my biggest critic and at the same time, my greatest supporter.

Bobbee Ferrer

AN INVITATION....

To the many great cooks and leaders in the racing industry who have favorite recipes they are willing to share, I have included a recipe form in the back of the book. I invite you to submit your special recipes to PROVEN PERFORMANCES II which, with your help, could become an even better collection of "Recipes From Thoroughbred Racing Leaders."

CONTENTS

Morning Workout

Breakfast Foods

Breads and Rolls

SECTION COVERS
BY
VIRGINIA NEARY

Virginia Neary is an internationally recognized artist. Her work is published in such magazines and newspapers as The Thoroughbred Record, Horseman's Journal, Spur, The Bloodhorse, The Thoroughbred of California, McCall's, Maryland Horse, N.Y. Times, London Times, and the Scottish Daily Express. Her paintings and drawings grace the collections of many prominent horsemen.

For six years Virginia was an owner and licensed trainer of Thoroughbreds in Louisiana. She has a great understanding and empathy for the horse which is reflected in her work. "It's the 'heart', the determination and courage, that I try to get in touch with through my drawings and paintings. There is a fire in the Thoroughbred that captures the imagination. And for every moment of fire there is a moment of peace. Horses are creatures that express their emotions. That is why we can identify with them. As an artist it is that emotion I seek to capture and share with you."

Virginia is one of the originators of the "Race Against MS" and has been the key to the rapid expansion of support from the Thoroughbred industry. She serves with Bill Shoemaker as a national spokesperson for this program.

WHOLE WHEAT PANCAKES

1 ⅓ cups whole wheat flour
2 teaspoons baking powder
¼ teaspoon salt
1 egg, slightly beaten
1⅓ cups milk
1 tablespoon brown sugar
1 tablespoon oil

Grease griddle (it is generally unnecessary to grease a well-seasoned griddle or one with a non-stick surface). Heat griddle while mixing batter. Griddle is hot enough when drops of water sprinked on it will bounce. Mix flour, baking powder and salt. Beat egg, sugar and oil together. Add liquid mixture to flour mixture. Stir only until flour is moistened. Batter will be slightly lumpy. For each pancake, pour about ¼ cup batter onto hot griddle. Cook until covered with bubbles and edges are slightly dry. Turn and brown other side. Serve with Blueberry Sauce.
Serves: 4, 2 pancakes each

BLUEBERRY SAUCE

2 teaspoons cornstarch
½ cup water
¾ cup frozen unsweetened blueberries, thawed and crushed
2 tablespoons honey
2 teaspoons lemon juice

Mix cornstarch with a small amount of water in a saucepan, stir until smooth. Add remaining water, blueberries and honey. Bring to boil over medium heat, stirring constantly. Cook until thickened. Remove from heat. Stir in lemon juice. Serve warm over whole wheat pancakes.
Serves: 4, ¼ cup each

Origin: *I Love America Diet,* by Phyllis George Brown
Favorite recipe of: Phyllis George Brown
Career Highlights: Married to John Y. Brown, former governor of Kentucky; former Miss America and currently co-host of the "CBS Morning News".

VIOLA'S LACY CORN CAKES

1 cup corn meal
½ teaspoon baking soda
½ teaspoon salt
1 egg, beaten
1-1¼ cups buttermilk

Mix corn meal, baking soda and salt together. Add the beaten egg and buttermilk, beating until smooth. The secret of having the cakes trimmed with lace is to get the batter thin enough. (Thin too thick buttermilk with milk or water.) Dip a good tablespoon of batter onto a hot griddle. Turn cake as soon as it browns. Don't stand by and "spank" the cakes after they have been turned. It is necessary to stir the batter each time before dipping or pouring.
Serves: 4-6

Origin: Mrs. Bell's mother's cook, Viola
Favorite recipe of: Mr. and Mrs. John A. Bell III, Jonabell Farm, Lexington, Kentucky

VON HEMEL'S GERMAN PANCAKES

3 eggs, slightly beaten
½ cup flour
¾ cup milk
Sugar and salt to taste

Mix all ingredients. Pour batter into hot buttered skillet. Brown on each side. Bake pancakes in a preheated 400° oven for 10 minutes. Serve with fresh-squeezed lemon juice and syrup.
Serves: 4

Origin: Mrs. Don (Roylynn) Von Hemel, Omaha, Nebraska
Favorite recipe of: Don Von Hemel, Trainer
Career Highlights: Trained the 1983 winner of the Cornhusker Handicap in Omaha, Nebraska, *Win Stat.* A new world record was set by *Win Stat* in the spring of 1984 at Oaklawn Park for one mile and 70 yards.

"Morning line — Forecast of probable odds."

PAIN PERDU
(Lost Bread)

½ loaf stale French bread, or 4 slices of any type bread
3 tablespoons butter
2 eggs
¼ cup milk
¼ teaspoon vanilla
1 tablespoon white sugar or honey

Mix eggs, milk, sugar and vanilla. Soak bread in mixture as you prepare pan. In frying pan, heat butter on medium heat. Do not allow butter to burn. Cooking time is about 1 minute on each side or until it is golden brown. Spinkle top with powdered sugar, or spread with syrup, honey or jelly.
Serves: 4

Origin: Raymond Salmen used to prepare this dish on Saturday mornings for his
              daughter, Sandra, before she went horseback riding.
Favorite recipe of: Sandra Salmen, Publicity Director, Fair Grounds,
                   New Orleans, Louisiana

CHOCOLATE TOAST

Sliced bread
Butter or margarine
Cocoa
Sugar

Spread soft butter or margarine thickly over bread. Using proportions of 1 cocoa to 3½ sugar, mix cocoa mixture. (Example: for one slice of bread, mix 1 teaspoon cocoa and 3½ teaspoons sugar.) Spoon mixture on center of buttered bread. Gently spread to cover entire slice. Broil at 425° until chocolate is bubbly, about five minutes. Careful, do not burn.
Serves: As many as desired

Original recipe of: Larry Speck, World Renowned Professional Gambler

EGGS SARDOU

4 artichoke bottoms
1 tablespoon chopped green onion
2 tablespoons butter
2 tablespoons flour
1 cup light cream
1 10-ounce package frozen chopped spinach, cooked and drained
2 teaspoons lemon juice
3 tablespoons Parmesan cheese
Salt and pepper to taste
4 eggs, poached
¾ cup Hollandaise sauce
Paprika

In a small saucepan, warm artichoke bottoms in salted water and place in a greased baking dish. In a separate saucepan, saute green onion in butter; blend in flour, stirring constantly. Gradually pour in cream and cook until thickened. Combine spinach, lemon juice, cheese, salt and pepper. Add to the cream sauce and mix well. Place ¼ of the spinach mixture on each artichoke bottom and keep warm in the oven. Poach eggs and place one egg on each filled artichoke bottom. Serve eggs immediately topped with Hollandaise sauce and sprinkle with paprika. The Hollandaise sauce may be kept warm by pouring it into a jar and placing the jar in warm water.
Serves: 2

HOLLANDAISE SAUCE

4 egg yolks
2 tablespoons lemon juice
½ pound butter, melted
¼ teaspoon salt

In top half of double boiler, beat egg yolks and stir in lemon juice. Cook very slowly in double boiler over low heat, never allowing water in bottom pan to come to a boil. Add butter a little at a time, stirring constantly with a wooden spoon. Add salt and pepper if desired. Continue cooking slowly until thickened.
Yield: 1 cup

Origin: Brennan's Restaurant, New Orleans, Louisiana
Favorite recipe of: The Editor

RICK'S SURE WINNER
(Omelette)

4 tablespoons butter, divided
4-ounce can sliced mushrooms
½ medium onion, chopped
5 eggs
½ cup milk
Salt and pepper to taste
¼ pound processed cheese, sliced thin
6 slices bacon, fried crisp & crumbled or ¼ pound
      smoked ham, chopped
Optional: ½ cup picante sauce

Melt two tablespoons butter in frying pan and saute mushrooms and onions until onions are soft. If using ham, saute with mushrooms and onions. In a bowl, wisk eggs and milk with salt and pepper. Heat a non-stick skillet over medium heat and add remaining butter. Pour egg mixture evenly into pan and cook over low heat until bottom of egg mixture is firm. Add remaining ingredients starting with cheese, then bacon or ham, onions and mushrooms. Fold omelette over with large spatula, wait 30 seconds and slide onto plate. Serve the picante sauce if desired.
Serves: 2

MOET CHANDON MIMOSA

Chilled Moet Chandon Champagne
Orange juice

Fill half of a large bowl-shaped wine glass with champagne, the other half with orange juice. Enjoy!

Origin: Frazier Family's home, Hot Springs, Arkansas
Favorite recipe of: Ricky Lee Frazier, Jockey
Career Highlights: Apprentice records held at Louisiana Downs: Most mounts ridden
      in a season, 1981; most wins in a day, 4; most wins in a season, 92;
      most stakes winners in a season, 8. Journeyman records held:
      Most winners in a single day, 7; most mounts ridden in a season,
      862; voted "Jockey of the Month" by Turf Publicists of America,
      October, 1984.

"Bug Boy — Apprentice jockey, because of asterisk with which newspapers identify apprentice in entry lists."

AT THE GATE BREAKFAST CASSEROLE
"Prepared the evening before"

Cheese Sauce:
2 tablespoons butter
2 tablespoons flour
1 cup milk
½ teaspoon salt
⅓ teaspoon pepper
1 cup shredded American processed cheese
Topping:
2½ cups soft bread crumbs
¼ cup butter
Casserole:
2 cups cubed, cooked ham
⅓ cup chopped green onions
3 tablespoons melted butter
1 dozen eggs, beaten
1 4-ounce can sliced mushrooms, drained
¼ teaspoon paprika

Prepare Cheese Sauce and Topping; set aside.
Cheese Sauce: Melt butter and stir in flour; cook until bubbly. Slowly add milk, stirring briskly. Cook until thick. Add salt, pepper and cheese and mix well.
Topping: Saute bread crumbs in butter until well blended.
To assemble casserole, saute ham and onions in melted butter in a large skillet. Cook until onions are tender. Add beaten eggs and cook over medium heat until soft set. Stir in mushrooms and cheese sauce. Place mixture in a flat 3-quart casserole. Spoon topping over egg mixture and sprinkle with paprika. Refrigerate overnight. When ready to bake, preheat over to 350° and heat for 30-35 minutes.
Serves: 12

Favorite recipe of: Marilynne Howsley Jacobs, Thoroughbred Owner, Albany, Texas

MOTHER'S DAY SPECIAL

2 tablespoons oil
2 cans tamales, halfed
1 can refried beans
Tortilla chips
2 cups grated Cheddar cheese
8 eggs, beaten and scrambled
Picante sauce, to taste

Evenly distribute oil on bottom of iron pot or large casserole dish. Place halfed tamales to cover bottom. Mix refried beans with enough water to make them spreadable and spread over tamales. Add a layer of tortilla chips and a layer of cheese, 1 cup. Distribute eggs evenly over cheese. Layer with another bunch of chips and the remaining 1 cup of cheese. Picante sauce may be added to taste. Bake at 350° until thoroughly heated, about 20 minutes.
Serves: 6

Origin: Original recipe developed one Mother's Day by Jim McCall
Favorite recipe of: Dr. Jim McCall, Ruston, Louisiana
Career Highlights: Developed the first complete Thoroughbred Racing Program at Louisiana Tech; developed the first complete Thoroughbred Breeding Management Program at the University of Maryland.

LIVELY BEER BISCUITS

4 cups biscuit mix
2 tablespoons sugar
1 teaspoons salt
1 12-ounce can beer

Mix all ingredients together and drop into greased muffin tins. Bake at 350° for 15 minutes.
Yield: 20 biscuits

Favorite recipe of: John Lively, Jockey, Pearcy, Arkansas
Career Highlights: Rider of 1976 Preakness winner, *Elocutionist;* won the Arlington-Washington Futurity on *Let's Don't Fight* in 1981. Leading rider at Omaha for eight years and leading rider at Oaklawn Park for two years.

"Hand ride — Urging horse toward longer, faster, more rhythmic stride by rolling hands on its neck, lifting its head at beginning of stride."

MAJESTIC LIGHT
"It is both!"

6-ounce can snow crab meat
2 tablespoons mayonnaise
¼ cup chopped water chestnuts or celery
¼ teaspoon dill weed
3 English muffins, 6 halves
1 large tomato
6 4-inch squares Jack cheese
Cayenne pepper, optional

Mix crabmeat, mayonnaise, water chestnuts or celery and dill weed. Place mixture on 6 lightly toasted muffin halves. On top of crabmeat mixture, place a slice of tomato and a slice of cheese. Sprinkle with cayenne pepper if desired and broil until cheese is melted.
Serves: 3, 2 muffins each

Origin: John's wife, Diane, developed this great recipe when "mucking out" the frig.
Favorite recipe of: John W. Russell, Trainer, Arcadia, California
Career Highlights: Trained over 60 stakes winners of over 100 stakes including *Susan's Girl* (Champion three times and winner of over $1,250,000), *Track Robbery* (Champion and millionaire), *Majestic Light, Intrepid Hero, Effervescing, Tri Jet,* and *Singh.*

WILLARD SCOTT'S RECIPE FOR CHEESE GRITS SOUFFLE

1 cup quick cooking grits
1 teaspoon salt
½ cup butter, separated
1 6-ounce roll Kraft's Garlic Cheese
2 eggs, beaten
¼ cup milk
Salt and pepper to taste
1 cup crushed corn flakes

Cook grits in 4½ cups water and salt. When done, stir in 6 tablespoons butter and garlic cheese (optional on the garlic). Allow to cool. Add beaten eggs and milk to grits and season with salt and pepper. Pour into buttered casserole dish. Mix corn flakes with remaining 2 tablespoons melted butter and sprinkle over grits. Cover well and bake at 350° for 40-45 minutes. DELICIOUS!
Serves: 6

Favorite recipe of: Willard Scott, TODAY Show, NBC News, New York, New York
Racing interests: Covers the Kentucky Derby and other major Thoroughbred racing events for NBC News.

CHEESY CHILI CASSEROLE

2 4-ounce cans sliced, green chilies
1 pound Cheddar cheese, grated
1 pound Monterey Jack cheese, grated
4 eggs
2 tablespoons flour
2 13-ounce cans evaporated milk
2 8-ounce cans tomato sauce

Butter a 9x13-inch casserole. Line dish with ½ of sliced chilies. Cover chilies with Cheddar cheese and add another layer of green chilies. Combine milk, eggs and flour in a bowl. Beat and pour over casserole. Next add half of the Monterey Jack cheese. Place in preheated 400° oven for 30 minutes, covered. Remove and add remaining cheese and cover with tomato sauce. Bake uncovered for 15 minutes. Good for brunch!
Serves: 8-10

Favorite recipe of: Mary Jo and Steve Gasper, Omaha, Nebraska
Career Highlights: Once worked at Walmac Farm in Lexington, Kentucky raising, boarding and training horses. Their son, John J. Gasper, represents jockey Keith Allen.

MORNING GLORY MUFFINS

4 cups all purpose flour
2½ cups sugar
4 teaspoons each baking soda and cinnamon
1 teaspoon salt
4 cups grated carrots
1 cup each raisins and chopped pecans
1 cup shredded coconut
2 apples, peeled and grated
6 large eggs
2 cups vegetable oil
4 teaspoons vanilla

In a large bowl, sift together flour, sugar, baking soda, cinnamon and salt. Stir in raisins, pecans, coconut and apples. In a separate bowl beat eggs with vegetable oil and vanilla. Stir egg mixture into the flour mixture until the batter is just combined. Spoon the batter into well-buttered ⅓ cup muffin tins, filling them to the top. Bake the muffins in a preheated 350° oven for 35 minutes or until they are springy to the touch. Let cool for about 5 minutes then turn out. These freeze very well. Take out as needed.
Yield: 30 muffins

Origin: Morning Glory Cafe in Nantucket
Favorite recipe of: John W. Records
Career Highlights: Assistant Racing Secretary at Oaklawn Park and Calder; Racing Coordinator for John Franks of Shreveport, Louisiana; Assistant Racing Secretary, Fonner Park.

"Morning Glory — Horse that runs well in workouts but not in races."

STOLLEN

1½ cups warm milk
4 tablespoons butter
⅓ cup sugar
1½ teaspoons salt
2 tablespoons dry yeast
2 eggs, room temperature
6 cups, unbleached flour, approximately
1½ cups mixed diced candied fruit; nuts, raisins, etc.
Nutmeg, fresh grated

Mix first 4 ingredients, add yeast and dissolve. Set aside about 5 minutes, then add eggs, flour and fruit. When dough is mixed, let rise until doubled. Form into 3 oval loaves and fold over like a Parker House roll. Place on a greased baking pan. Brush with butter and sprinkle with nutmeg. Let rise again. Bake at 350° for 35 minutes.
Yield: 3 loaves

Origin: A German bread very popular in Louisville at Christmas.
        This is Laurie Lussky's version.
Favorite recipe of: Bill and Laurie Lussky, owners of Belmont Farm, Louisville, Kentucky

BEFORE FOAL BREAD

1 cup milk
½ cup margarine
¼ cup sugar
1 teaspoon salt
1 package dry yeast
3½ cups flour
1 cup melted margarine

Combine milk, margarine, sugar and salt in pan. Heat until margarine melts. Cool and add yeast, stir until dissolved. Place flour in large bowl, add milk mixture, stir until blended. Cover and let rise about 1 hour and 20 minutes (or until doubled in size). Roll into 1 1 2-inch balls, dip into melted margarine, layer balls in 10-inch tube pan, cover and let rise until doubled in size (approximately 45 minutes). Bake at 375° for 35 minutes. Cool in pan 5 minutes and invert onto serving plate.
Yield: One round loaf

Favorite recipe of: Bennett Heft, Robstown, Texas
Racing interest: Bennet Heft writes, "Thoroughbred racing is my hobby and
                  interest. General contracting is my business. My father-in-law, the
                  late Jack Spurlock who raised and raced thoroughbreds always said
                  he would get even with me for marrying his daughter. He did — he
                  left me a mare! That was 30 years ago and many horses later. My wife
                  and I race in Louisiana, New Mexico and Mexico. We really
                  love racing."

"Foal — Newborn horse; of a mare, to give birth."

DAY BREAD

½ cup warm water
1 package dry yeast
2 tablespoons butter
1 cup milk
1 teaspoon salt
1 tablespoon sugar
4-4½ cups flour

Stir together water and yeast and let set until bubbles form, about 10-15 minutes. Mix butter, milk, salt, sugar and 1½-2 cups flour (just enough flour to make dough workable). Put in buttered bowl, turn once, place in a warm spot and let rise until doubled in size. Punch down and work in 2½ cups more flour. Knead 7-10 minutes. Again, put in buttered bowl, turn, place in warm spot and let rise until doubled. Knead again, then let dough rest about 5 minutes. Divide and put in 2 buttered bread pans. Let rise in warm spot for about 15 minutes. Bake at 350° for 1 hour. Bread tops can be brushed with butter the last 15 minutes of baking.
Yield: 2 loaves

Origin: Frona Day, Springfield, Missouri.
        Mrs. Sam (Jill) Maple's great-grandmother. It won many blue ribbons at fairs.
Favorite recipe of: Sam Maple, Jockey, Hot Springs, Arkansas
Career Highlights: Asked to represent the United States in the International
                   competition held in South Africa in 1979.

TRACK RECORD ROLLS

2 packages dry yeast
1 teaspoon sugar
¼ cup warm water
1 cup melted butter
1 cup milk
½ cup sugar
2 beaten eggs
½ teaspoon salt
4 cups flour

Sprinkle 1 teaspoon sugar on top of yeast and dissolve in warm water. Mix together butter, milk and ½ cup sugar. Add eggs, salt, flour and yeast mixture. When blended, place in greased bowl. Cover and chill overnight. Roll out and form into rolls. Brush tops with butter or margarine. Let rise about 2½ hours. Bake at 400° until lightly browned, about 10 minutes.
Yield: 24-30 rolls

Favorite recipe of: Jockeys Julio Espinoza and Larry J. Melancon, Louisville, Kentucky
Editor's Note: I received this recipe from Kim Espinoza and Becky Melancon,
              the wives of Julio and Larry. Both are excellent cooks and the best
              of friends. It is not surprising that they would submit the same recipe.

THE GREATEST YEAST ROLL RECIPE EVER

1 package dry yeast
1 tablespoon sugar
2 cups water
¼ cup sugar
1 teaspoon salt
¼ pound butter (½ cup)
1 egg
4+ cups flour

Mix yeast, 1 tablespoon sugar and 1 cup warm water. Set aside 5 minutes until it bubbles. Combine 1 cup water, ¼ cup sugar, salt and butter; mix well and add egg, then yeast mixture. Add flour, enough to make it easy to handle. Knead 5-7 minutes. Put in buttered bowl and let rise until double in size. Punch down, knead again. Separate into rolls, place in pan and let rise until double in size. Bake at 350° until golden, about 10 minutes. Brush with butter.
This same recipe is also great for **Cinnamon Rolls:**

Dough recipe
4 tablespoons melted butter
½ cup sugar
5 teaspoons cinnamon
Frosting:
1 box powdered sugar
¼-½ cup milk
1 tablespoon butter
1 teaspoon vanilla

After kneading dough second time, roll out to ¼ inch thickness. Melt butter and spread over dough. Sprinkle with mixture of sugar and cinnamon. Roll up like a jelly roll and cut into ½ inch slices. Place on cookie sheet and let rise about 20 minutes and bake as above. Frost with mixture of powdered sugar, milk, butter and vanilla.
Yield: 24-30 rolls

Origin: Lottie Jester, Hot Springs, Arkansas
Favorite recipe of: Sam Maple, Jockey, Hot Springs, Arkansas
Career Highlights: Riding six winners in one day, including the stake race at
                    Ak-Sar-Ben.

BANANA BREAD

2 cups flour
½ teaspoon baking powder
1 teaspoon baking soda
½ teaspoon salt
½ cup oil
½ teaspoon vanilla
1 cup brown sugar
2 eggs
4 large, ripe bananas, mashed
1 cup pecans or walnuts, chopped

Grease an 8x4x2-inch loaf pan. Combine all dry ingredients. Cream sugar and oil until fluffy. Add eggs, one at a time, and vanilla. Stir in bananas. Add flour in four portions, beating until smooth after each addition. Turn into prepared pan. Bake at 350° for about 50 minutes or until toothpick inserted in center comes out clean.
Yield: 1 loaf

Origin: Mrs. Steve (Ellen) Chiasson
Favorite recipe of: Steve Chiasson, Trainer, Benton, Louisiana

BANANICOT BREAD

1½ cups flour
¼ cup wheat germ
2¼ teaspoons baking powder
⅓ cup butter
⅔ cup sugar
¾ teaspoon grated lemon rind
2 beaten eggs
1 cup ripened banana pulp
½ cup chopped pecans or walnuts
¼ cup chopped apricots

Sift together flour and baking powder. Stir in wheat germ. Cream sugar and butter, then add lemon rind. Mix in beaten eggs and banana pulp. Add dry ingredients and beat for 3 minutes. Fold in nuts and apricots and pour into greased bread pan (8½ x 4½). Bake in a preheated 350° oven for 1 hour. Freezes well.
Yield: 1 loaf

Origin: Old 1931 cookbook from Louisville, Kentucky
Favorite recipe of: Sam Maple, Jockey, Hot Springs, Arkansas
Career Highlights: The first jockey to win the Omaha Gold Cup and Cornhusker Handicap (Ak-Sar-Ben's 2 biggest races) back to back within one week (1976) on *Joachim* and *Dragset*.

A SURE WINNER
(Olive-cheese bread)

3 cups biscuit mix
2 tablespoons sugar
1 egg
1½ cups buttermilk
1 cup stuffed olives, drained & sliced
1 cup grated Swiss cheese

Combine first 4 ingredients. Mix until blended. Gently stir in olives and cheese. Pour into 9x5x3-inch loaf pan. Bake in preheated 350° oven for 50-55 minutes. Can also be baked in 3 small loaf pans. Keep refrigerated after serving. This bread freezes well.
Yield: 1 large or 3 small loaves.

Favorite recipe of: Peggy McReynolds, Bedford, Texas
Career Highlights: "Owning *Explosive Wagon* and seeing (I'm always there but I keep my eyes closed) the "Wagon" run in the Kentucky Derby and Super Derby. Just being a small part of the racing industry is a big highlight in my life."

PUMPKIN BREAD

½ cup milk
½ cup salad oil
½ cup sugar
½ cup brown sugar
1 teaspoon salt
3½ cups flour
1 package dry yeast
2 eggs
3 cups cooked pumpkin
1 teaspoon cinnamon
1 teaspoon nutmeg
½ cup raisins
½ cup chopped walnuts

Combine milk, ½ cup water (may substitute additional milk for water), oil, sugars, salt in small saucepan. Heat over low heat until mixture is just warm. Measure 1½ cups flour, and yeast and mix until blended, about 30 seconds. Add warm milk mixture to flour and yeast. Beat with mixer until smooth. Add remaining flour, eggs and pumpkin. Beat until smooth. Add cinnamon and nutmeg. Beat until well blended. Stir in raisins and walnuts. Pour into 2 small loaf pans that have been greased (I use Pam). Let dough rise for about 1 hour. Be sure to cover dough with waxed paper and then with a kitchen towel. Bake in preheated 375° oven for 30 to 35 minutes or until brown. Let cool about 10 minutes before removing from pans.
Note: Oven should be preheated for 10 minutes before the dough is placed inside. This allows the yeast to expand.
Yield: 2 loaves

Origin: Ryan Haase, New Orleans, Louisiana
Favorite recipe of: The Editor

STROMBOLI

Processor Italian Bread
3¼ cups all purpose flour
1 tablespoon sugar
1 teaspoon salt
1 tablespoon butter
1 package dry yeast
1 cup + 2 tablespoons very warm water
Cornmeal
Vegetable oil
1 egg white
1 tablespoon water

Combine 2 cups flour, sugar, salt, butter and yeast in bowl of processor. Using metal blade, process until butter is cut into dry ingredients. Add ½ cup water and pulse 4 times. Add 1 cup flour and remaining water. Pulse 4 times and process until ball of dough forms. If dough is too sticky, add remaining flour, 1 tablespoon at a time. When proper consistency, let processor run an additional 40-60 seconds. Cover bowl and let rest for 20 minutes. Roll dough into 10x15-inch rectangle. Fill and layer with Strombolli filling.

Filling
1 green pepper, thinly sliced
1 yellow onion, thinly sliced
2 tablespoons margarine
½ pound pepperoni, thinly sliced
½ pound mozzarella cheese, grated
¼ cup Romano cheese, grated

Saute onions and peppers in margarine until soft. Drain. Heat pepperoni on low to remove excess oil. Drain. Toss together onions, peppers, pepperoni and mozzarella cheese. Sprinkle ¼ cup Romano cheese on bread dough. Distribute onion mixture evenly over cheese. Additional cheese may be added if desired. Beginning at wide end, roll tightly, jelly roll style. Place on greased baking sheet sprinkled with cornmeal. Rub with vegetable oil and cover with plastic wrap. Refrigerate 2-24 hours.
When ready to bake, remove plastic wrap and let stand at room temperature for 10 minutes. Make 3-4 slits on top of loaf. Bake at 425° for 20 minutes. Remove bread from oven and brush with mixture of egg white and water. Bake 5-10 minutes longer or until golden brown.
Serves: 4

Favorite recipe of: Patrick Pope, Racing Secretary, Louisiana Downs,
            Bossier City, Louisiana

In The Paddock

Beverages

Appetizers

Pastas

EGGNOG

4 eggs
⅓ cup sugar
⅛ teaspoon nutmeg
⅛ teaspoon salt
1 teaspoon vanilla
1 drop lemon flavoring
4 cups very cold milk
½ cup very cold cream

Beat eggs until thick and lemon colored. Add sugar, nutmeg, salt, vanilla and lemon flavoring. Add milk and cream and beat until frothy. Sprinkle nutmeg on each serving of eggnog.
Yield: 6 large glasses

Origin: Mrs. M. H. Van Berg, Jack's mother, used to prepare this eggnog for his dad after they had finished a big cattle sale at their Sales Pavillion in Columbus, Nebraska. Jack used to work at the cattle sales as a young boy and later auctioned the sale.
Favorite recipe of: Jack Van Berg, Goschen, Kentucky
Career Highlights: Winner of the Eclipse Award as North America's champion trainer in 1984. Inducted into Racing's Hall of Fame in 1985.

STARTING GATE BLOODY MARYS

1 quart tomato juice
1 quart tomato cocktail
½ teaspoon salt
⅛ teaspoon pepper
Dash of hot sauce
Dash of Worcestershire sauce
Dash of celery salt
1½ cups vodka
Celery stalks

Combine first 7 ingredients, mixing well; chill overnight. Stir vodka into tomato juice mixture; pour over ice cubes, if desired. Garnish with celery stalks.
Yield: 9 ½-cups

Favorite recipe of: Jacque Hefte, Thoroughbred Owner, Robstown, Texas

"Bolt — To run off in wrong direction, as when horse tries to return to barn instead of going to the starting gate."

CAPE COD

Vodka
Cranberry juice
Grapefruit juice
Slice of lime

Pour vodka (about 1 ounce per drink) over ice in glass. Add 4 ounces cranberry juice and 1 ounce grapefruit juice. Garnish with a twist of lime. Very refreshing.

Origin: Ben Butler, Shreveport, Louisiana.

RED ROOSTER

1 2-quart bottle cranberry juice
1 large can frozen, concentrated orange juice
2 cups vodka

Mix and freeze in a plastic container overnight. Serve in Champagne glasses. Mixture will be slushy. Great for parties.
Serves: 8-10

Favorite recipe of: The Editor

COFFEE PUNCH

1 cup sugar
1 gallon hot, strong coffee
1 teaspoon vanilla
2¼ quarts vanilla ice cream, cut in 1-inch chunks
1 pint cream
Variation: Part chocolate and/or coffee flavored ice cream may be used
                   with vanilla.

Stir sugar into hot coffee, then chill thoroughly. Combine coffee with ice cream and vanilla. Pour into punch bowl and add cream.
Serves: 25-30

Origin: A friend in the St. James Episcopal Church in Dalhart, Texas.
Favorite recipe of: Phil and Marilyn Like, Dalhart, Texas
Racing interests: Thoroughbred owners and racing enthusiasts.

JUNEAU'S KAHLUA

2 ounces Antique Instant Coffee
4 cups sugar
2 cups boiling water
1 whole vanilla bean (½ inch long)
2 cups (plus) Brandy, least expensive you can buy
2 wine bottles
2 corks

Stir sugar and boiling water until dissolved; add coffee. Cut vanilla bean in half and put each half in a wine bottle. To each bottle add 1 cup brandy and half of the coffee mixture; then fill with brandy. Cork bottles and store in a dark closet for at least 30 days. This makes great Christmas gifts that you can prepare well in advance!
Yield: 2 bottles

Origin: Old family recipe
Favorite recipe of: Tommie Juneau, Dallas, Texas
Racing interests: Thoroughbred owner and racing enthusiast.

OFFICIAL KENTUCKY DERBY MINT JULIP

Silver mugs or collins glasses
Powdered sugar
Water
Ice bucket full of finely crushed ice
Old Kentucky Tavern Bourbon Whiskey
Fresh mint

For each drink:
Dissolve 1 teaspoon powdered sugar with 2 teaspoons water into silver mug or collins glass. Fill with crushed ice and add 2 ½ ounces bourbon. Stir until glass is heavily frosted adding more ice if necessary. (Do not hold glass with hand while stirring). Decorate with five or six sprigs of fresh mint so that the tops are about two inches above rim of mug or glass. Use short straws so that it will be necessary to bury nose in mint. The mint is intended for odor rather than taste.

Origin: Mr. Boston Deluxe Official Bartender's Guide
Submitted by: Phillip Roberts, Glenmore Distilleries Company, Louisville, Kentucky
          Mr. Roberts is the Louisiana State Manager of Glenmore Distilleries
          Company, distributors of Kentucky Tavern Bourbon, used to make
          the OFFICIAL KENTUCKY DERBY MINT JULIP.

TAYLOR TEA

6 tea bags
3 lemons
2 scant cups sugar or to taste
1 gallon plus 1 quart water

Wash lemons and roll with palm on cabinet to break down pulp. Measure sugar in large pot. Put lemons and tea bags in quart saucepan, fill with water and bring to steam stage (do not boil). Remove tea bags and place in a strainer over sugar, gently squeeze bags. Pour hot tea and lemons from saucepan on top of sugar and stir to dissolve sugar. Add half of cold water to hot tea. Cut lemons in half, squeeze lemons, stir in remaining water. Taste for sweetness. Strain into two ½ gallon jars and refrigerate.
Serves: 10 or more

Origin: Old family recipe
Favorite recipe of: The Taylor Family, Mr. & Mrs. Joseph L. Taylor,
                     Duncan, Ben, Frank & Mark, Taylor Made Farm,
                     Nicholasville, Kentucky

HOT SPICED TEA

3 sticks cinnamon
1 tablespoon whole cloves
3 large or 6 small teabags
1 large can frozen concentrated orange juice
1 small can frozen concentrated lemonade
¾ cup sugar
1 large bottle gingerale
1 gallon container

In a teapot, steep cinnamon sticks, cloves and teabags in boiling water for 30 minutes. In a gallon container, add tea mixture, orange juice, lemonade, sugar and gingerale and enough water to make one gallon. Serve hot! "Can also be refrigerated, in fact it gets better. Serve it cold after a day at the races. You can add a little vodka or whiskey, if you like."
Yield: 1 gallon

Origin: Old Family recipe.
Favorite recipe of: Tommie Juneau, Dallas, Texas
Racing interests: Thoroughbred owner and racing enthusiast. When Tommie is not at
                   the races, she can be found in the Dallas Market where she sells
                   high fashion clothing.

HOT NUTS

3 tablespoons red pepper
3 tablespoons olive oil
4 cloves garlic, crushed
1 12-ounce can cocktail nuts
1 12-ounce can Spanish peanuts
1 teaspoon chili powder
1 teaspoon garlic powder

Heat red pepper in oil for 1 minute. Add crushed garlic to oil. Add nuts and cook over medium heat for 5 minutes stirring often. Remove from heat and drain nuts on paper towel. Sprinkle chili powder and garlic salt over nuts. Cool completely and store in air tight container. Good with drinks.
Yield: 3 cups nuts

Origin: Mrs. J. E. (Mary Lynn) Anthony
Favorite recipe of: John Ed Anthony, Fordyce, Arkansas
Racing interest: Owner of Loblolly Stable; owned *Cox's Ridge,* winner of eleven
stakes; owner of *Temperence Hill* who won the Belmont Stakes,
Travers, Jockey Gold Cup, Super Derby, Eclipse Award in 1980.

BENEDICTINE

1 small cucumber
1 small onion
1 8-ounce package cream cheese
Green food coloring

Peel cucumber and remove seeds. Peel and quarter onion. Put both in processor and grind. Drain well. Discard juice or use for soup. Place drained pulp back in processor with cream cheese and blend well. Add a drop or 2 of green food coloring. Store in a glass jar in refrigerator and use for sandwiches or canapes. Especially good on dark bread.
Yield: 8½ ounces

Origin: Iennie Benedict, a Louisville cateress at the turn of the century.
Favorite recipe of: Bill and Laurie Lussky, Louisville, Kentucky
Career Highlights: Owners of Belmont Farm in Belmont, Kentucky. Parents of four
daughters, Caroline (23), Edie (22), and Ann Boyd (18) and
Frances (15).

"Dark horse — Underrated animal that wins or has good prospects of winning."

PICKLED QUAIL EGGS

1 dozen quail eggs
1 small onion, chopped
¼ cup vinegar
½ cup water
Dash salt and pepper

Hard boil eggs, approximately 15 minutes. Peel eggs and place in a bowl. In a saucepan, combine onions, vinegar, water, salt and pepper. Bring this mixture to a boil. Pour the hot pickling solution over the eggs until they are completely covered. Store in the refrigerator. Serve chilled.

Favorite recipe of: Bennett Parke, Director of Racing, Detroit Race Course

HOT ARTICHOKE DIP

1 can artichoke hearts, chopped
1 cup mayonnaise
1 cup grated Parmesan cheese
Garlic powder to taste

Mix ingredients. Put in ramekin or small casserole dish. Heat for 20 minutes at 350° or until bubbly. Serve with chips.
Serves: 4

Favorite recipe of: John Ed Anthony, Fordyce, Arkansas
Career Highlights: Owned *Cox's Ridge* who won eleven stakes races in his 3-4 year-old year.

ARMADILLO DIP DELUXE

1 ripe armadillo
½ pint sour cream
1 small diced tumbleweed
4 green chilies
1 teaspoon prairie dog
1 pinch ground horny toad

Peel armadillo, saving shell. Add diced tumbleweed, green chilies, prairie dog, horny toad and smash together with your hand. Add sour cream and mix well. Place dip in armadillo shell which has been pre-oiled with hind quarter of jack rabbit.
To add to your dining pleasure, serve with coffee, spiced liberally with tequila and garnished with mesquite leaves. (Mesquit-a-rita)

Favorite recipe of: Rick Brasher, Trainer, Arkansas and Louisiana
B.S. For information on how to catch ripe armadillos on the hoof, contact Rick Brasher.

DELAHOUSSAYE VEGETABLE DIP

⅔ cup sour cream
⅔ cup mayonnaise
1 tablespoon chopped parsley
1 tablespoon chopped green onions
1 tablespoon dill weed
1 tablespoon finely chopped garlic
1 tablespoon Accent
10 drops Tabasco Sauce

Mix all ingredients together and refrigerate for 2 hours. Serve with raw vegetables.
Yield: 12 ounces

Origin: Mrs. Eddie (Juanita) Delahoussaye
Favorite recipe of: Eddie Delahoussaye, Jockey, Arcadia, California
Career Highlights: Rider of the 1982 and 1983 Kentucky Derby winners,
     Gato del Sol and *Sunny's Halo.*

CLAM DIP CLAIMER

1 8-ounce package cream cheese
2 tablespoons clam juice
1 6½-ounce can minced clams
Juice of 1 lemon
1 tablespoon Worcestershire sauce
Dash Tabasco

Drain 2 tablespoons clam juice from canned clams and combine with softened cream cheese. Stir until creamy. Drain remaining juice from clams and discard. Add clams, lemon juice, Worcestershire sauce and Tabasco to cream cheese mixture and blend well. Serve with corn chips or raw vegetables.
Variation: Substitute 1 4½-ounce can shrimp for clams and 2 tablespoons milk for clam juice. Makes a great Shrimp Dip.
Yield: 1½ cups

Favorite recipe of: The Editor

"Claimer — Claiming race; horse that runs in such a race."

J. J.'S GUACAMOLE DIP

2 ripe avocados, reserving 1 seed
1 large tomato, chopped and seeded
4 green onions, chopped
½ fresh jalapeno pepper, chopped
¼ teaspoon powdered lemon, or juice of ½ lemon
Garlic salt, to taste
Lemon pepper, to taste

Using a potato masher, mash avocados well. Stir in remaining ingredients. Place seed in center of dip to prevent avocados from turning brown. Serve with tortilla chips.

Favorite recipe of: J. J. Pletcher, Trainer, Benton, Louisiana
Career Highlights: Trained over 30 stakes winners including *Uncool, Circle of Steel, Lockjaw, Double Line, Breaker Breaker* and *Limited Edition.*

OLIVARES' "ALWAYS A WINNER" TACO TO GO

1 10½-ounce can bean dip
3 avocados, ripe
Salt and pepper to taste
1 teaspoon lemon juice
Pinch garlic salt
1 tablespoon Mexican salsa
1 8-ounce carton sour cream
1 12-ounce jar thick, mild taco sauce
1 cup shredded Cheddar cheese
Optional: 1 chopped tomato, ½ cup chopped scallions, 1 small
           can sliced olives

Spread bean dip on bottom of a 3-inch deep, 8-inch round or square glass pan. In a small bowl, mash avocados with salt, pepper, lemon juice, garlic salt and salsa to make guacamole. Spread guacamole over bean dip. Spread sour cream over the guacamole. (try to keep layers from mixing together). Pour and gently spread taco sauce over sour cream layer. Sprinkle grated cheese over taco sauce and add any or all of the optional toppings. Serve with tortilla chips.

Origin: Mrs. Frank (Gina) Olivares
Favorite recipe of: Frank Olivares, Jockey, Sierra Madre, California
Career Highlights: 1982 Florida Derby, rider of *Little Reb* who beat Affirmed at Santa Anita in 1978; 1977 George Woolf Award recipient.

FARRIER'S BAR CHEESE

2-pound box processed cheese
1 5-ounce jar horseradish
9 tablespoons mayonnaise or salad dressing

Melt cheese over very low heat. Remove from heat, blend in horseradish and mayonnaise. Stir until smooth. Serve on crackers. Store in air tight containers. Keeps for months in refrigerator. Can be frozen and used later. "Quick and tastes great."
Yield: 4 8-ounce containers

QUICK NACHO CHEESE DIP

2-pound box processed cheese
1-2 jalapeno peppers, chopped
¼ cup chopped black olives
¼ cup chopped pimentos
1 small onion finely chopped
1 small can evaporated milk
Nacho chips

Melt cheese in crock pot with milk. Add chopped jalapeno, olives, pimentos and onion. (olives and pimentos are added primarily for color - add more or less to your taste.) Stir and keep on low heat. Use as dip or cover nacho chips in individual bowls. Left over dip may be refrigerated and remelted on stove over low heat, or in microwave.
Serves: 20

Origin: Mrs. Richard (Dawn) McChesney
Favorite recipe of: Richard A. McChesney, Louisville, Kentucky
Career Highlights: Third generation blacksmith who works primarily on the
Keeneland and Churchill Downs tracks and the Miami area
tracks in the winter.

"Farrier — Blacksmith."

MRS. JULIAN G. ROGERS' CHEESE LOAF

1 pound sharp Cheddar cheese, grated
1 cup pimentos, drained and chopped
½ cup mayonnaise
½ teaspoon red pepper
½ teaspoon salt
1 tablespoon vinegar
1 cup chopped nuts
1 envelope Knox gelatin, mixed with 1 cup VERY HOT water

Mix all ingredients except the nuts and gelatin. Mix well, then add nuts. Add gelatin and work well with hands until thoroughly mixed. Put in a 2-quart mold and chill for several hours. Invert onto serving plate and serve with crackers.

Favorite recipe of: Mrs. Julian G. (Margaret) Rogers, Paris, Kentucky
Career Highlights: Owner of Idle Hour Farm in Paris, Kentucky. Mrs. Rogers
has been the breeder of several outstanding horses, as *Ribocco* and *Ribero* (back to back full brothers that won both the Irish Sweeps Derby and The St. Leger Stakes in 1967 and 1968) and *Roses For The Star* (winner of the Houghton Stakes and second in the Epsom Oaks).

PHOTO FINISH FROMAGE

1 8-ounce package cream cheese, softened
10-12 small green onions, chopped fine
2 teaspoons Worcestershire sauce
2 packages shredded, dried or chipped beef

Mix all ingredients together using ½ beef. Roll into a ball. Then roll ball into rest of beef. Freeze or store in refrigerator until ready to use. Serve with crackers.

Favorite recipe of: Julio Espinoza, Jockey, Louisville, Kentucky
Career Highlights: Won the Phoenix Handicap, the oldest stake race in the country, four times in a row at Keeneland Race Course.

"Photo finish — A race so closely contested that the winner must be determined by a photograph taken of the finish."

CHEESE BISCUITS

1½ pounds sharp Cheddar cheese, shredded
¾ pound butter
3 cups flour
½ teaspoon salt
1 teaspoon red pepper

Cream cheese and butter. Sift flour with salt and pepper. Blend together cheese and flour. Roll into 1-inch balls. Chill for several hours or overnight. Place on cookie sheet and bake for 12-15 minutes at 400°.
Yield: 4 dozen

Favorite recipe of: The Editor

JALAPENO FUDGE

1 pound Longhorn cheese, shredded
4 fresh jalapeno peppers, seeded and chopped
4 eggs, beaten

Mix cheese and peppers together and pour beaten eggs over mixture. Mix and pour into 9x9-inch square casserole (ungreased). Bake in 400° oven for 20 minutes or until golden brown around edges. Cut into squares and serve on tortilla chips.
Serves: 6-8

Favorite recipe of: Richard and Sandra Fox, Albany, Texas
Racing interests: Owners of Live Oak Ranches, the Foxes initially raced
Quarter Horses, but Thoroughbreds are their present racing interest.

HOT PEPPER LOG

1 tablespoon butter
1 3-ounce package softened cream cheese
8 ounces sharp pasturized American cheese, shredded
¼ teaspoon finely crushed red pepper flakes
1 tablespoon chopped green pepper
1 tablespoon chopped red pepper
Optional: ½ cup chopped pecans or sliced almonds

Mix cheeses and butter together with mixer at medium speed until well blended. Add green and red peppers, pepper flakes and beat well. On a sheet of waxed paper, form into 7-inch log. Wrap and chill at least 4 hours. Remove from refrigerator about 30 minutes before serving. Optional: May be rolled in nuts at this point. Serve with assorted crackers.
Yield: 7-inch log

Favorite recipe of: Judy Cooper, Equine artist, Tree Line Thoroughbred Farm,
Elm Grove, Louisiana

JUDY COOPER

A working farm manager of her own Tree Line Thoroughbreds, Judy Cooper finds time for doing portraiture of her greatest passion, the Thoroughbred. Her work is included in the private collections of many distinguished owners, trainers, jockeys and race enthusiasts in the US and Canada.

Each year Ms. Cooper paints the finish of the previous year's Super Derby race, with the original watercolor donated to the National Kidney Foundation of Louisiana, to be auctioned at the Super Derby - Kidney Foundation Ball. Proceeds from the painting go to this very deserving Foundation so that many will benefit from the race long after the cheers on Super Derby Day.

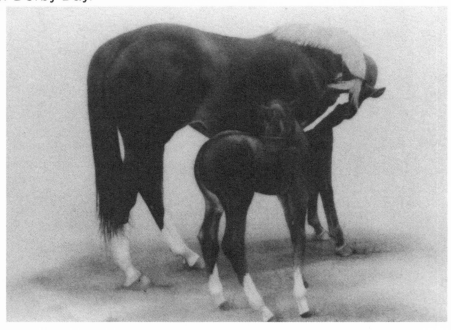

JUDY'S CARROT SANDWICHES

2 cups shredded carrots, packed
1 8-ounce package softened cream cheese
2 tablespoons mayonnaise
1 teaspoon fresh lemon juice
Creole seasoning, to taste

Mix all ingredients together in a small bowl and let stand in the refrigerator, covered for at least 1 hour. Serve on small slices of Pumpernickle bread, open faced. This is great on an hors d'oeuvre tray.
Yield: 25-30 sandwiches

SPINACH BITES
WITH LEMON MAYONNAISE

1 10-ounce package frozen, chopped spinach, thawed and drained
1 cup herb-seasoned stuffing mix
2 eggs, lightly beaten
½ cup grated Parmesan cheese
⅓ cup melted butter
Dash of ground nutmeg
1 teaspoon minced onion

Lightly grease cookie sheets. Mix above ingredients until well blended. Shape into balls using a teaspoon of mixture for each ball. Place on baking sheets, cover and chill for at least 4 hours (or freeze until ready to bake). Preheat oven to 350°. Bake spinach bites for 10 minutes or until bottoms begin to brown. Spear warm bites with toothpicks and dip in Lemon Mayonnaise.

Lemon Mayonnaise

½ cup mayonnaise
1 teaspoon sugar
1 teaspoon Dijon mustard
1 tablespoon fresh lemon juice
Dash Tabasco sauce
¼ cup sour cream

In a small bowl, mix mayonnaise, lemon juice, mustard, hot sauce and sugar until smooth. Stir in sour cream. Serve as dip for Spinach Bites.
Yield: About 65 bites

Favorite recipe of: Judy Cooper, Equine artist, Tree Line Thoroughbred Farm,
Elm Grove, Louisiana

RAW KIBBI

1 cup Burgol (Fine No. 2 Cracked Wheat)
2 pounds ground meat
1 medium Spanish onion, chopped
Salt, to taste
1 teaspoon black pepper
1 teaspoon cinnamon
1 teaspoon nutmeg
Paprika
2 tablespoons olive oil

Soak cracked wheat in cold water for 10 minutes, then drain. Add ground beef, onions, salt, pepper, cinnamon, nutmeg and mix very well for 5 minutes or until thoroughly blended. Serve in a large platter. Sprinkle with paprika and pour olive oil over all. Can be served with fine Lebanese Pita bread or with crackers. Can be prepared early and refrigerated.
Serves: 6-8

Origin: Nafla Sefa's Lebanese recipe
Favorite recipe of: Farid Sefa, Brighton, Michigan
Career Highlights: Owner of *Sefa's Beauty,* winner of the 1985 Grade I Apple
                 Blossom Handicap.

ALMOST KIBBI

1 cup cracked wheat, finely ground
2 pounds raw, coarsely ground round steak (all fat and gristle removed)
2 egg yolks
½ cup finely chopped onions
4 mashed anchovies
To taste:
Salt and pepper
Capers
Chopped parsley and herbs
Worcestershire sauce
Olive oil
1 sprig fresh mint, crushed, if available

Rinse wheat in pan of water. Drain water by cupping hands and squeezing out all moisture. Add wheat to ground meat, egg yolks, onions, anchovies, and remaining seasonings to taste. Mix well and serve in individual plates. A teaspoon of good olive oil poured over each serving is delicious.
Serves: 6

Origin: George Ackel, who claims that his version of Kibbi takes the
       "raw meat" taste away.
Favorite recipe of: George J. Ackel, Thoroughbred Owner, Harahan, Louisiana

BOURBON HOT DOGS

1 cup brown sugar
1 cup ketchup
1 tablespoon grated onion
½ cup bourbon
1 package hot dogs, cut into bite-sized pieces

Combine first 4 ingredients in a sauce pan and heat slowly on top of stove. Add hot dogs and simmer until completely heated, about 20-30 minutes. Microwave instructions: Combine first 4 ingredients in a glass container. Cook 2 minutes at medium heat, then rotate container ¼ turn and stir sauce. Cook 2 minutes on high heat. Stir in hot dogs and cook 1 minute on high heat. Serve in chafing dish with toothpicks.
Serves: 6-8

Favorite recipe of: Ted Kuster, Paris, Kentucky
Career Highlights: Owner-Manager Westview Farm, thoroughbred breeding operation; past president Kentucky Thoroughbred Farm Managers Club; T.C.A.; breeder of several stakes winners.

HOT CHIPPED BEEF

2 8-ounce packages cream cheese
4 tablespoons milk
Tabasco Sauce, good shake
6 ounces chipped beef, shredded
½ chopped onion
1 cup sour cream
½ cup finely chopped green pepper
½ teaspoon black pepper
½ teaspoon salt
1 cup chopped pecans, browned in butter

Soften cream cheese with milk. Mix with all ingredients except nuts. Put in ramekin or small casserole dish and top with nuts. Bake at 350° for 20 minutes. Spread on crackers.
Serves: 12

Origin: Mrs. J. E. (Mary Lynn) Anthony
Favorite recipe of: John Ed Anthony, Fordyce, Arkansas
Career Highlights: Owned *Cox's Ridge* who won 11 stakes his 3-4 year old year. *Temperence Hill* won Belmont Stakes, Travers, Jockey Gold Cup, Super Derby, Eclipse Award in 1980 as Champion 3-year old colt.

CHICKEN WINGS IN SOY AND HONEY

3 pounds chicken wings
Black pepper, to taste
2 tablespoons vegetable oil
½ cup soy sauce
2 tablespoons ketchup
1 cup honey
1 clove garlic, chopped

Preheat oven to 375°. Cut off and discard wing tips of chicken wings. Cut the remaining wings in two parts and sprinkle with pepper. Combine remaining ingredients and pour over chicken wings in a greased baking dish. Bake for 1 hour until well done and sauce is carmelized. If chicken starts to burn, reduce heat. May be served with rice and a vegetable as a main course or alone as an appetizer. Delicious!
Serves: 6 as main course, or a party of 20.

Favorite recipe of: Tony Bently, New Orleans, Louisiana
Racing interest: Track Announcer, Fair Grounds

CHICKEN LIVER PATE

½ pound butter, divided
1 pound chicken livers
½ clove garlic, finely minced
¼ small onion, chopped
⅛ teaspoon basil
2 tablespoons cognac
Salt and pepper to taste

Melt ¼ pound of butter in a skillet. Saute livers quickly until brown on the outside, but still pink in the middle, about 5 minutes. Cool until butter starts to set. Cover pan and turn livers several times to prevent darkening. Place livers in blender. Add remaining ingredients. Blend until smooth, pushing down with a spatula. Adjust seasoning and put in a well-buttered 1-quart mold. Cover and refrigerate overnight. Serve on toasted French bread rounds.
Optional: ⅛ pound fresh mushrooms, chopped, 2 tablespoons butter, Saute mushrooms in butter until tender, about 3 minutes. Fold into pureed pate and mold as usual.
Serves: 8-10

Favorite recipe of: Joe Ferrer, Jockey Agent, New Orleans, Louisiana

"Jockey agent — Person who helps rider obtain mounts in return for 25 percent or more of the rider's earnings."

ROMERO'S MARINATED CRAB CLAWS

1 bunch green onions (tops and bottoms) chopped
½ cup celery, chopped
4 pods garlic, minced
1 cup fresh parsley, chopped
2 cups Spanish olive oil
2 cups Tarragon vinegar
Juice of 6 lemons
2 tablespoons salt
1 tablespoon pepper
1 teaspoon garlic powder
1 package dry Italian salad dressing

Chop green onions by hand; all other vegetables are easier in a processor. Mix all ingredients together. Let stand at room temperature for 48 hours. Spoon marinade over boiled crab claws. Also excellent with boiled shrimp!
Yield: Approximately 5 cups

Origin: Mrs. Gerald (Mona) Romero
Favorite recipe of: Randy Romero, Jockey, New Orleans, Louisiana
Career Highlights: One of only two jockeys (Terry Lipham is the other) to ride
in both the Kentucky Derby and the All-American Futurity; only
rider to win titles at all five Louisiana racetracks; won riding titles
at Keeneland (twice) and Churchill Downs in Kentucky and
Arlington Park (1982), setting a record for wins at the Chicago track.

CRAB CANAPES

½ cup margarine
1 5-ounce jar cheese spread
½ teaspoon mayonnaise
½ teaspoon seasoned salt
½ teaspoon garlic salt
1 6½-ounce can crabmeat, drained
9 English muffins, split

Mix margarine, cheese, mayonnaise, salts and crabmeat together. Spread on muffins and freeze in single layer. Cut each muffin into six pie-shaped pieces; wrap and store in freezer. Just before serving, broil until lightly brown.
Yield: 108 bite-size appetizers

Origin: Origin: Mrs. Cloyce K. (Fern) Box
Favorite recipe of: Cloyce K. Box, Frisco, Texas
Racing interest: Thoroughbred owner and racing enthusiast.

OYSTER PATTIES

2 onions, finely chopped
1 bunch green onions, chopped
½ pound fresh mushrooms, chopped
1 pint oysters, chopped
Salt, pepper and cayenne, to taste
¼ cup margarine
1 10½-ounce can cream of mushroom soup
2 tablespoon cream
2 tablespoons Kitchen Bouquet
2 slices Muenster cheese
2 tablespoons chopped parsley
4 dozen miniature patty shells

Saute onions in margarine until tender; add green onions, mushrooms, oysters and simmer for 15-20 minutes. Add seasonings, soup, cream and Kitchen Bouquet. Simmer for an additional 10 minutes. Add cheese broken into small pieces and parsley. Stir until cheese is melted and well blended. Fill patty shells with mixture. Heat in 375° oven for about 10-12 minutes or thoroughly heated.
Yield: 4 dozen patty shells

Favorite recipe of: The Editor

CENTER CIRCLE SHRIMP

3 pounds shrimp
6 tablespoons melted butter
2 teaspoons celery salt
3 tablespoons lemon juice
Mayonnaise, approximately ½ cup

Boil and peel shrimp. Puree in food processor adding butter, celery salt, lemon juice and as much mayonnaise as needed to make a nice, smooth paste (should be quite thick). Press into 2-cup mold and chill. Garnish with whole shrimp and fresh parsley. Serve with crackers.

Origin: Original recipe of Mrs. Frank (Judy) Behler
Favorite recipe of: Frank Behler, New Orleans, Louisiana
Career Highlights: Among the top 10 leading trainers in the nation in 1963. Now a director on the board of the Horsemen's Benevolent and Protective Association, serving for 18 years, longer than any other board member.

VINCENT'S BARBECUED SHRIMP

2 cups margarine
5-6 cloves garlic, finely minced
2 whole bay leaves
2 teaspoons rosemary
½ teaspoon basil
½ teaspoon oregano
½ teaspoon salt
½ teaspoon cayenne pepper
½ teaspoon nutmeg
½ teaspoon paprika
5 tablespoons freshly ground pepper
Juice of 4 lemons
3 pounds whole fresh shrimp, including heads
1 lemon, thinly sliced

In a saucepan, melt margarine. Add all other ingredients except shrimp and sliced lemon. Cook over medium heat for a few minutes allowing flavors to blend. In a large baking pan, combine shrimp and heated sauce. Bake at 350° for 15 minutes; turn shrimp, sprinkle with more pepper if desired, place lemon slices on top of shrimp and bake for an additional 15 minutes. Serve at once with hot French bread.
Serves: 4-6

Original recipe of: Vincent Timphony, New Orleans, Louisiana
Career Highlights: Former owner of Vincenzo's Restaurant in New Orleans,
          Louisiana; trainer and part owner of *Wild Again*,
          winner of the Inaugural Breeder's Cup Classic.

SALMON TO SHOW

1 8-ounce can salmon
1 3-ounce package cream cheese
2 tablespoons horseradish
Juice of ½ lemon
1 cup fresh parsley, chopped
½ cup pecans, chopped fine

Mix salmon, softened cream cheese, horseradish and lemon juice in small bowl. Chill for about 2 hours. Mix parsley and pecans together. Make salmon mixture into a ball and roll in parsley and pecan mixture. Serve with lemon wedges and crackers.
Yield: 12-ounce ball

Origin: Mrs. John (Linda) Records
Favorite recipe of: John W. Records
Career Highlights: Assistant Racing Secretary at Oaklawn Park and Calder
          Race Course; Racing Coordinator for John Franks,
          Shreveport, Louisiana; presently Assistant Racing Secretary
          at Fonner Park, Grand Island, Nebraska.
"Across the board — Three bets (win, place and show) on one horse."

VAN BERG DELIGHT

12 large shrimp or baby lobsters tails, peeled
Flour
½ cup butter
1 tablespoon chopped garlic
1 tablespoon chopped green onion
Ground black pepper and salt to taste
4 ounces dry white wine
1 tablespoon chopped fresh parsley
Juice of ½ lemon

Lightly flour shrimp or lobster tails. Melt 2 tablespoons butter in large skillet over low heat. Add garlic, green onions and shrimp or lobster. Season with salt and pepper and stir constantly. Add 2 more tablespoons butter and cook shrimp or lobster about 5 minutes or until done. Take shrimp or lobster out of pan leaving as much butter in pan as possible. Add lemon juice, wine and stir with wooden spoon smashing garlic and onion. Stir until sauce starts to thicken. Add about 2 more tablespoons butter and stir until butter is heated. Remove from heat and add shrimp or lobster and parsley and stir until coated with thickened sauce. Serve immediately.
Serves: 4

Origin: A favorite restaurant in Pasadena, California
Favorite recipe of: Jack Van Berg, Goschen, Kentucky
Career Highlights: WInner of the Eclipse Award as North America's champion trainer of 1984. Eight times winner for most victories nationally; Preakness winner with *Gate Dancer* in 1984; in 1983, the only American trainer to win 4,000 races. 1985 inductee into Racing's Hall of Fame.

SPAGHETTINI CONTESSA

This is an elaboration of a popular Southern Italian sauce called *puttanesca* which means, in polite English, "in the manner of streetwalkers." Tom Ainslie dubs his version "contessa" on the supposition that his changes have moved the dish up in class. "Like most Neapolitan dishes, this one permits a lot of tinkering," he goes on. "You can vary the proportions to suit yourself. But the ingredients must be of the highest quality or you waste your time. For example, you ruin the dish if you use California olives or run-of-the-mill domestic pasta."

½ pound good, imported spaghettini
Imported olive oil, enough to cover the bottom of 8 or 10-inch skillet
6½ ounce can tuna fish, thoroughly drained of packing liquid
7 or 8-ounce can whole, peeled Italian plum tomatoes, drained
3-4 medium cloves of garlic, smashed, peeled and chopped fine
Plenty of black pepper, preferably from a pepper mill
Red pepper flakes or Tabasco or a chopped, seeded fresh Jalapeno,
    to taste
Salt to taste
Handful of Italian parsley, chopped
Half a handful of fresh, chopped basil, if you can get it
Generous teaspoon of dried oregano
10-12 Greek black olives or Italian ones such as Gaeta. (These must
    pitted and chopped very coarsely.)
2-3 tablespoons of imported large capers, carefully rinsed and drained
3-4 decent anchovies if you can find them, otherwise, don't bother

Put 3-4 quarts of slightly salted water to the boil. When it shows signs of approaching boil, put the olive oil over high heat, reducing it to medium and adding the chopped garlic when bubbles begin to form. Stir with a wooden spoon. When garlic begins to change color, add the tuna, break it up with the spoon, stir, and add the tomatoes, breaking them up. When well blended, add salt, as many grindings of black pepper as look good to you, the red pepper or its alternative, the oregano and the optional basil. Stir. Reduce heat to low. When the water boils, drop in the pasta, stir and test at intervals until it has almost reached the state of tenderness you prefer. At that point, add the parsley, olives and capers to the sauce. Stir carefully. When the pasta is done, dump it into a colander, drain well but do not rinse, then deposit in a large, heated bowl. Add the sauce, Mix. A green salad and any loud red wine go great with this.
Serves: 2

Favorite recipe of: Tom Ainslie, Millwood, New York
Career Highlights: Tom Ainslie's books about the art of handicapping are the all-time
                best sellers in that field. He also is a hard-knocking cook who
                specializes in emphatic flavors. Otherwise, he lectures, goes racing
                and maintains a low profile. As befits his standing as a grandfather,
                he is over 21.

AGLIO-OLIO

1 pound thin spaghetti
½ cup olive oil
2 cloves garlic, finely chopped
1 teaspoon freshly ground pepper
1½ teaspoons fresh, chopped parsley
2 cups steamed clams with juice
2 tablespoons butter

Cook spaghetti according to package directions. This should be boiling while preparing oil mixture. Heat oil in a deep fry pan. Add garlic, black pepper and parsley. When garlic is lightly browned, add clams and heat to a foamy appearance. Add clam juice. When ready to come to a boil, remove from heat. Drain spaghetti and toss with butter in a deep bowl. Pour oil and clam mixture over spaghetti. Get a loaf of fresh Italian bread, a jug of wine and enjoy!
Serves: 6

Origin: Tony "Bonesy" Cappola
Favorite recipe of: Darrel Haire, Jockey, Arcadia, California
Career Highlights: Rode *Temperence Hill* to victory in the Arkansas Derby in 1980.

SPAGHETTI CARBONARA

½ pound bacon, chopped in small pieces
4 eggs, beaten
¼ cup milk
½ teaspoon salt
Pepper, to taste
½ pound spaghetti
Parmesan cheese

Fry bacon until crisp. Keep warm. Pour off all but about 6 tablespoons drippings. Beat eggs, milk, salt and pepper in bowl and set aside. Cook spaghetti as desired. Drain spaghetti and immediately add to bacon with reserved bacon drippings. Add the egg mixture and stir thoroughly. The heat from the spaghetti cooks the eggs. Put on a warm platter and sprinkle with Parmesan cheese. Serve immediately.
Serves: 4

Origin: Rome, Italy
Favorite recipe of: Steve and Mary Jo Gasper, Omaha, Nebraska
Career Highlights: Raising, breeding and training horses at
                    Walmac Farm in Lexington, Kentucky.

HOMEMADE LINGUINE WITH WHITE CLAM SAUCE

Linguine:
1¾ cups flour
3 egg yolks
1 whole egg
2 tablespoons water
1 teaspoon olive oil
½ teaspoon salt
White Clam Sauce:
1 cup butter
2 cloves garlic, minced
½ bay leaf, crumbled
¼ cup chopped parsley
Salt and pepper to taste
1 6-ounce can minced clams
Parmesan cheese, freshly grated

Using a pasta maker, add flour and 1 egg at a time while mixing. Add other ingredients and continue mixing. Follow directions on pasta maker regarding length of time to knead. Using a linguine plate, cut noodles to desired length. Cook noodles in boiling water approximately 3 or 4 minutes depending on desired doneness. For clam sauce, melt butter in saucepan and add garlic, bay leaf, parsley, salt and pepper. Mix thoroughly and add clams and clam juice. When sauce is very hot, pour over well drained linguine and toss well. Serve immediately and sprinkle with Parmesan cheese.
Serves: 6

Favorite recipe of: Dr. Edward P. Giammarino, Glendale, California
Racing interest: An Optometrist by profession, Ed Giammarino is an avid race fan and excellent cook. He and his wife enjoy having dinner parties for their many friends in racing. This is one recipe that is always a big hit.

PASTA WITH CLAM SAUCE AND BROCCOLI

4 tablespoons butter
2 garlic cloves, chopped
1 6-ounce can chopped clams
2 cups chicken stock
4 egg yolks, beaten lightly
4 tablespoons heavy cream
¼ cup Parmesan cheese, more for topping
Red pepper and salt to taste
Broccoli florets, 1 bunch fresh or 2 boxes frozen
1 pound thin spaghetti

Steam broccoli to crisp-tender stage and set aside. Saute garlic lightly in butter. Add clams and stir 1 minute. Add chicken stock and cook an additional 2 minutes. Add all other ingredients except broccoli and stir until egg yolks thicken. Add broccoli and stir gently until heated. Pour over spaghetti (cooked al dente and drained) and sprinkle with Parmesan cheese. (Optional: Can omit clams and just use broccoli.)
Serves: 6

Favorite recipe of: John Ed Anthony, Fordyce, Arkansas
Career Highlights: Owned *Cox's Ridge,* winner of eleven stakes races; owned
  Temperence Hill, winner of Belmont Stakes, Travers, Jockey
  Gold Cup, Super Derby, and Eclipse Award in 1980 as champion
  3-year old colt.

CRAWFISH FETTUCCINI

4 tablespoons chopped green onions
1 tablespoon minced garlic
1 pound fresh, sliced mushrooms
½ cup butter
1 pint whipping cream
1 pound crawfish tails
1 teaspoon seafood seasoning
¼ cup white wine
1 pound fresh fettuccini
Fresh parsley and lemons for garnish

In a large skillet, saute onions, garlic and mushrooms in butter for 5 minutes. Add cream, crawfish tails, seasoning and wine. Cook, stirring occasionally, until well blended and thoroughly heated. Cook fettuccini to al dente stage. Drain well. Toss fettuccini with sauce. Serve on heated plates garnished with fresh parsley and lemon wedges.
Variation: Shrimp, crabmeat or scallops may be substituted for crawfish, but crawfish is best.
Serves: 6-8

Favorite recipe of: Cliff Rednour, New Orleans, Louisiana
Career Highlights: Thoroughbred owner, former Racing Secretary, Jefferson
  Downs, Kenner, Louisiana.

SPINACH, MUSHROOMS AND CREAM WITH SPAGHETTI

4 cups shredded, fresh spinach leaves
½ pound fresh mushrooms
Juice of one lemon
4 tablespoons butter
1 clove garlic, chopped fine
2 tablespoons Marsala wine or dry sherry
1 cup heavy cream
Freshly ground black pepper
½ pound spaghetti
Freshly grated Parmesan cheese

Cook the spinach in boiling water until tender; 5 minutes should do it. Drain thoroughly and set aside. Wipe the mushrooms with a damp towel to clean and cut off stem ends; slice thin, add lemon juice and mix well. Melt butter in a skillet and add the garlic and Marsala. Cook for 3 minutes, then add mushrooms. Cook an additional 5 minutes and add the cream and bring the mixture to a boil. Add some fresh ground pepper and remove from heat. Cook the spaghetti until al dente (firm). Drain and return to the pot in which it was cooked. Add first the cooked spinach, then the mushroom mixture to the pasta. Toss and serve with Parmesan cheese.
Serves: 2 as a main course, or 4 as an appetizer

Favorite recipe of: Tony Bently, New Orleans, Louisiana
Career Highlights: Announcer for the Budweiser Million on NBC in 1983; Track Announcer at the Fair Grounds since 1974; calling *Spectacular Bid's* return to the races for ABC television.

"Walkover — A race from which all but one horse are scratched, permitting the horse to win by walking the distance."

SPINACH LASAGNE SWIRLS

16 packaged lasagne noodles
2 10-ounce packages frozen chopped spinach, thawed
2 cups (6-ounces) grated Parmesan cheese
2 ⅔ cups ricotta cheese
1 teaspoon each salt and pepper
½ teaspoon ground nutmeg
2 cloves garlic, pressed
1 large onion, chopped
3 tablespoons olive oil or salad oil
2 15-ounce cans tomato sauce
¼ cup dry red wine
½ teaspoon each dry basil and oregano leaves

Cook noodles according to package directions. Drain, rinse with cold water, and drain again. Squeeze spinach to remove excess moisture. In a bowl, mix spinach with 1½ cups Parmesan cheese. Add ricotta, salt, ½ teaspoon of the pepper, and nutmeg; mix together. Spread about ¼ cup of this cheese mixture along entire length of each noodle; roll noodle up. In two buttered 9x13-inch baking pans, place each rolled noodle on end so they do not touch. In a frying pan over medium heat, cook garlic and onion in olive oil until onion is soft. Add tomato sauce, wine, basil, oregano, and the remaining ½ teaspoon pepper. Simmer, uncovered for 10 minutes. Pour sauce over and around noodles. Bake, covered, in a 350° oven for about 30 minutes or until heated through. Remove from oven and sprinkle lasagne evenly with remaining ½ cup Parmesan cheese. Can be made ahead and refrigerated or frozen. "I usually bake half and freeze the other for another meal."
Yield: 16 swirls

Favorite recipe of: The Editor "These pinwheels are as pretty as they are delicious."

Post Parade

Soups

Salads

Salad Dressings

WATERCRESS SOUP

BUCKINGHAM PALACE

1 ounce butter
1 ounce flour
1 pint chicken stock
2 bunches fresh Watercress, about 6 ounces
½ pint single cream

Melt the butter, add flour and cook for a couple of minutes on low heat, stirring gently. Slowly add warmed chicken stock until you have a creamy consistency. Wash the watercress thoroughly and add to the mixture. Cook slowly until the stalks are soft, stirring occasionally. This will take about 20 minutes. Remove from heat and allow to cool. Liquify the soup in a blender or food processor and pass through a fine sieve. Chill and add the cream. Reserve a little of the cream to garnish the top of each portion. A few leaves of Watercress, previously blanched, can provide additional garnish if wanted.
Serves: 3

Favorite recipe of: Prince Charles and Princess Diana,
The Prince and Princess of Wales
Buckingham Palace, London, England

Racing interest: The Royal Family's enthusiasm for the sport
has done much to elevate the public
image of Thoroughbred racing worldwide.

CREAM OF BRUSSELLS SPROUT SOUP

2 cups brussels sprouts, coarsely chopped
3 cups homemade chicken stock
2½ tablespoons butter
2 tablespoons flour
1½ cups light cream
Salt to taste
Pepper to taste
Worcestershire sauce to taste

Cook sprouts in the stock over medium heat until tender. Puree the sprouts and stock. Melt butter in soup pot and blend in flour, then stir in cream. Simmer over low heat, stirring constantly until thickened. Stir in the pureed mixture and simmer three minutes; DO NOT BOIL. Season and serve.
Serves: 4

Origin: Adapted from The New York Times Bread and Soup Cookbook
Favorite Recipe of: Ronald E. Waggoner, M.D., Thoroughbred Owner Omaha, Nebraska

GET THE GREEN
(Lettuce Soup)

2 large heads lettuce
1 medium onion, chopped
4 cups milk
2 tablespoons butter
2 tablespoons flour
Salt and pepper to taste
For Liaison: 2 egg yolks
      3 tablespoons heavy cream
For Garnish: 1 cup bacon, fried and chopped
      Fried croutons

Wash lettuce thoroughly and shred. In a sauce pan, melt butter and add lettuce and onion. Cover with buttered paper and pan lid. Cook over low heat 8-10 minutes. Remove from heat and stir in flour. Scald milk and blend in lettuce mixture. Simmer very gently with lid off for 10 minutes. If soup is boiled hard it will curdle. Puree soup in blender and return to clean sauce pan and heat. Immediately add Liaison.
Liaison: Mix egg yolks and cream in a bowl. Add a little hot soup and stir this mixture into remaining soup which you have removed from the heat. Cook over low heat until soup thickens. Taste for seasoning and pour into heated tureen.
Garnish with bacon. Serve with croutons in a separate bowl.
Serves: 6 1-cup servings

Favorite recipe of: Judy A. Behler
        New Orleans, Louisiana
Career highlights: Owner and breeder of *Judy's Diamond,* a race mare
        who won 4 of her first 5 starts. She is a stakes winner
        of over $125,000. In 1984 she defeated Horse
        of the Year, *Monique Rene* at the Fair Grounds

TURNIP SOUP FOR TWO

2 large pork chops
Salt and pepper to taste
2½ quarts water
1 small rutabaga turnip
2 tablespoons corn meal
Sugar to taste

Salt and pepper pork chops. Put them in a soup pot with the water and cook until tender, about 30-40 minutes. Remove pork chops and debone. Cut meat into bite size pieces and set aside. Cook turnips in pork broth until tender, about 15-20 minutes. Remove from liquid and mash. Return meat and turnip to broth. Bring to a boil and slowly sprinkle in corn meal and sugar. When slightly thickened, soup is ready to eat.
Delicious served with HOT WATER CORN BREAD!
Serves: 2

Favorite recipe of: Roger Smith, Thoroughbred Owner, Stephens, Arkansas

CHUPE DE CAMARONES
(Shrimp Soup)

2 pounds fresh shrimp, peeled
2 tablespoons corn oil
1 teaspoon minced garlic
1 teaspoon coarsely ground red pepper
Salt, to taste
1 beef bouillon cube
1 cup corn
1 cup cooked rice
1 cup green peas
4 potatoes, cut in small pieces
1 13-ounce can evaporated milk

Heat corn oil in a large pot over medium heat. Add the garlic, red pepper, salt and bouillon cube and cook for 3 minutes. Add 6 cups of water, corn, rice, peas and potatoes and let boil gently for 20 minutes. Add the shrimp and evaporated milk and stir to heat evenly, about 4-5 minutes. Serve at once.
Serves: 6

Origin: Elsa Valdizan's mother from Lima, Peru.
Favorite recipe of: Fernando Valdizan, Trainer, Bossier City, Louisiana
Career Highlights: Fernando enjoyed a successful riding career before turning his interests to training. He presently trains his horses in Louisiana and Arkansas.

PUNTER'S POT SOUP
(Leek and Potato Soup)

¾ pound leeks, about 3 large
1 stalk celery
½ cup butter, separated
1 quart water
1 quart chicken broth
2 pounds potatoes, peeled and diced
½ cup heavy cream
Salt, white pepper to taste

Chop leeks (including tops) and celery finely. Melt ¼ cup butter and add leeks and celery. Reduce heat, cover and cook for 5 minutes or until leeks "sweat". Do not fry. Add water and broth, potatoes and salt and pepper to taste. Simmer 45 minutes or until leeks and potatoes are very soft. Put vegetables through sieve and return to pot. If too thick, add more chicken broth. Just before serving, add remaining ¼ cup butter and heavy cream and heat through. Do not boil.
Serves: 8

Origin: La Parisienne, Monrovia, California
Favorite recipe of: John W. Russell, Trainer, Arcadia, California
Career Highlights: Trained over 60 stakes winners of over 100 stakes include *Susan's Girl* (champion thre times and winner of over $1,250,000), *Track Robbery* (champion and millionaire), *Majestic Light, Intrepid Hero, Effervescing,*

"Punter — An English term for gambler, horseplayer."

FLEECED LAMB SOUP

2 lamb shanks
1 tablespoon rosemary
½ teaspoon seasoned salt
½ teaspoon freshly ground pepper
1 tablespoon flour
⅛ pound hot bulk pork sausage
3 strips thick bacon
1 large onion, chopped
1 cup fresh mushrooms, sliced
1 large carrot, chopped
1 large stalk celery, chopped
1 quart homemade stock, lamb, chicken or beef
½ cup cauliflower, chopped
½ cup parsley, chopped
1 medium potato, peeled, chopped
3 large cloves garlic, chopped
1 14-ounce can Italian tomatoes, chopped
1 tablespoon Worcestershire sauce
½ teaspoon Tabasco
½ cup dry red wine
Parmesan cheese to taste

Place lamb shanks in shallow pan and sprinkle both sides with rosemary, salt, pepper and flour. Brown in a 400° oven for 1 hour, turning 2-3 times.

Heat a soup pot. Place sausage and bacon in pot. After 2 minutes add onion and saute 3 minutes. Add mushrooms and saute 3 minutes. Add celery, potato and carrot and saute 3 minutes. Add stock, cauliflower, parsley, tomatoes with juice, Worcestershire sauce, Tabasco and wine.

Remove lamb shanks from pan, place in pot and discard fat. Deglaze the pan with water and add to pot. Bring to a boil, then reduce heat and simmer 2 hours. Sprinkle parmesan cheese on surface of each serving. May be prepared in advance, in fact, improves with age.
Serves: 6

Original recipe of: Ronald E. Waggoner, M.D., Thoroughbred Owner Omaha, Nebraska
Career Highlights: "Dr. Waggoner says he has no highlights yet. This may be true on the racetrack, but I'll bet he gets rave reviews in the kitchen!"

TORTILLA SOUP

¼ cup chopped onion
1 tablespoon olive oil
1 clove garlic, pressed
1 16-ounce can whole tomatoes
¾ cup vegetable juice cocktail
1 can beef broth
½ cup water
2 tablespoons picante sauce
1 teaspoon Worcestershire sauce
1 teaspoon sugar
½ teaspoon chili powder
½ teaspoon ground cumin
2 corn tortillas, 6 inches each
Dairy sour cream or sharp Cheddar cheese, shredded

In a 2-quart saucepan, saute onion in oil for 5 minutes over medium heat until golden. Add garlic and cook and stir for 1 minute then remove from heat. Puree tomatoes in a blender then add to onion mixture in saucepan along with vegetable juice, broth, water, sugar, picante sauce, cumin, Worcestershire sauce, and chili powder. Return pan to heat and bring to a boil. Reduce heat to low and simmer uncovered for 15 minutes. Cut tortillas into 1-inch stripes, then into triangles. Stir into hot mixture and simmer for 10 minutes. To serve, ladle soup into small bowls and top each serving with about ½ tablespoon sour cream or shredded sharp Cheddar cheese. Serve right away.
Serves: 6 2/3-cup servings

Favorite recipe of: Judy Cooper, Elm Grove, Louisiana
Career Highlights: Judy is a very talented Equine Artist. She and her husband Blanton W. Cooper are the owners of Tree Line Farm in Elm Grove, Louisiana.

TERRY'S MUSHROOM SOUP

4 tablespoons margarine
1 pound (4 cups) fresh mushrooms, sliced or chopped
1 cup chopped onions
2 tablespoons cornstarch
4 cups milk, divided
½ teaspoon pepper
2 chicken bouillon cubes

Melt margarine in a skillet over medium heat. Add mushrooms and onions and saute stirring frequently for 5 minutes or until tender. Stir together cornstarch and 1 cup of milk until smooth. In a medium saucepan, mix together cornstarch mixture and mushroom mixture, pepper, bouillon cubes and the remaining 3 cups of milk. Bring to a boil over medium heat, stirring constantly and boil for 1 minute. Serve immediately, or can be made several hours before serving and reheated.
Serves: 6

Origin: Mrs. Joe (Terry) King
Favorite recipe of: Joe King, Trainer, Louisville, Kentucky

SARATOGA ONION SOUP

4 cups sliced onions
½ teaspoon sugar
½ cup butter
1 tablespoon vegetable oil
1 clove garlic, minced
2 tablespoons flour
¼ teaspoon dry mustard
¼ cup Cognac
2 cups beef stock
2 cups chicken stock
1 can consomme
½ teaspoon nutmeg
⅛ teaspoon black pepper
½ teaspoon Worcestershire sauce
½ cup vermouth
6 slices toasted French bread
1 cup shredded Swiss cheese
1 cup shredded Monterey Jack cheese

Brown onions, sugar and butter in oil. Add garlic and cook 3 minutes. Sprinkle flour and mustard over onions, cooking and stirring 3 minutes. Raise heat and pour heated Cognac over top. Ignite and allow to burn off. Add remaining ingredients except vermouth, bread and cheese. Simmer 20 minutes. Refrigerate overnight. Re-heat and add vermouth just prior to serving. Pour into soup crocks and top each with a slice of toasted French bread and Swiss and Monterey Jack cheese. Put under broiler until cheese bubbles. Serve immediately.
Serves: 6

Origin: Original recipe of Ginny Howard, Lexington, Kentucky
Favorite recipe of: Neil A. Howard
Career Highlights: Manager of Eaton Farms, Inc. for Lee Eaton, Neil's cooking expertise is pretty much limited to the gas grill. Lucky for him, his wife, Ginny, is an excellent cook. Neil's career highlights was foaling, raising, and selling *Saratoga Six* for $2.2 million. But, as racing luck goes, after confirming his brilliance on the track with four straight wins (including a Grade I), he fractured sesamoids and will begin his stud career at North Ridge Farm in Lexington, Kentucky in 1985.

SHRIMP AND OKRA GUMBO

2 pounds fresh okra, sliced
1 medium onion, chopped
1 bell pepper, chopped
2 ribs celery, chopped
2 tablespoons cooking oil
1 8-ounce can tomato sauce
1 quart water
2-3 pounds shrimp, peeled
Salt, black and red pepper to taste
2 cups cooked rice

Mix okra, onion, bell pepper and celery in cooking oil and smother for 45 minutes over medium-low heat or until okra is cooked. Add tomato sauce and water. Add shrimp and season to taste. Cook an additional 15 minutes. Serve over rice.
Serves: 6-8

Original recipe of: Glyn P. "Tee Red" Bernis, Lafayette, Louisiana native

CAJUN GUMBO

1 cup cooking oil
½ cup flour
1 large onion, chopped
2 ribs celery, chopped
1 bell pepper, chopped
1 clove garlic, chopped
3 quarts boiling water
Salt and pepper to taste
2 ducks, cut in serving pieces
1 chicken, cut in serving pieces
½ pound smoked sausage, cut in ½ inch rounds
2 cups cooked rice

In a large heavy pot, heat ½ cup oil over medium heat. Add the flour, stirring constantly, until dark brown. Add onion, celery, bell pepper and garlic and cook until tender. Add the boiling water and season with salt and pepper. Season ducks and chicken pieces and fry until brown, turning occasionally. Transfer the pieces and pan scrapings to the gumbo. Simmer uncovered over low heat for 2½ hours or until the meat is tender. More water may be added if needed. Correct seasoning. Serve over rice in gumbo bowls.
Serves: 8

Favorite recipe of: Glyn P. "Tee Red" Bernis, Louisiana native
Career Highlights: Leading jockey in 1964; leading trainer at Louisiana Downs
for 2 years.

NEW ENGLAND CLAM CHOWDER

1½-inch thick piece salt pork, cut in small pieces
1 medium onion, thinly sliced
2 10½-ounce cans minced clams, reserve liquid
2 cups pared and diced potatoes
1 teaspoon salt
¼ teaspoon pepper
1 cup water
1 quart scalded milk
2 tablespoons butter

Cook salt pork until crispy and brown; drain on paper towel. Saute onion in drippings; pour off fat. Drain clams and combine with pork bits, onion, clam liquid, potatoes, salt, pepper and water in large saucepan. Cover and simmer about 10 minutes or until potatoes are just tender. Add clams, scalded milk and butter. Cover; set aside for 1-2 hours to blend flavors. Reheat; do not boil. If necessary, thicken with flour. Serve with crackers.
Serves: 6

Origin: Tony "Bonesy" Cappola
Favorite recipe of: Abigail Fuller, Jockey, New England Native
Career Highlights: Regular rider of *Mom's Command,* winner of the New York Filly
                    Triple Crown (Acorn, Mother Goose and Coaching Club
                    American Oaks), 1985

"Sex allowance — Weight concession that is given to female horses in races against males."

HOME STRETCH CAESAR

1 large head Romain lettuce
⅛ tube anchovy paste
1 coddled egg (boiled 1 minute)
1 large clove garlic, minced
Worcestershire sauce, dash or 2
Juice of 1 lemon
Dry mustard, couple of dashes
Salt and pepper to taste
¼-½ cup grated Parmesan cheese
Wine vinegar, dash
⅓ cup salad oil
½ cup croutons

Wash and drain lettuce leaves and chill. In a wooden or glass bowl, mix anchovy paste and egg. Add 1 ingredient at a time mixing well after each addition. Mix all ingredients except croutons to make dressing. Break leaves into pieces and add to salad bowl. Add croutons and toss well. Enjoy!
Serves:6

Favorite recipe of: Lynn A. Mason
Racing interest: Operates *Purple Onion Catering* in Hot Springs, Arkansas and wherever else her trainer-husband, Terry, takes her. The birth of their twin sons in May, 1985 may slow Lynn down a bit, but race trackers always look forward to her delicious delicacies.

"Homestretch — Straight part of track from final turn to finish wire."

SEVEN LAYER SALAD

1 head lettuce, chopped
1 head cauliflower, chopped
2 cups mayonnaise
1 medium onion, chopped
1 pound bacon, cooked and crumbled
⅓ cup Parmesan cheese
⅓ cup sugar

Layer in order given in a salad bowl. Cover and chill for 24 hours or overnight. Toss just before serving.
Serves:8-10

Favorite recipe of: Mr. and Mrs. Ted Kuster
Career Highlights: Theodore R. Kuster is owner-manager of Westview Farm in Paris, Kentucky, thoroughbred breeding operation; past president Kentucky Thoroughbred Farm Managers Club; T.C.A.; breeder of several stakes winners.

CYNTHIA'S SEVEN FURLONG SALAD

"This is a great company recipe that can be fixed the day before."
1 large green pepper, chopped
1 bunch scallions, chopped
1 head iceberg lettuce, shredded
1 bag frozen petit pois peas
1 16-ounce jar mayonnaise (may substitute diet mayo)
8 ounces Swiss cheese, shredded
1 pound bacon, cooked and crumbled
1 box cherry tomatoes, approximately 20-24
Straight sided, glass salad bowl is best to show layering

Mix green pepper and scallions and place in bottom of bowl. Layer finely shredded lettuce on top of scallions. Layer frozen peas, then cover thickly with mayonnaise, then shredded cheese. At this point, cover with plastic wrap and refrigerate overnight. Just before serving, layer crumbled bacon on top and ring outer edge with tomatoes. Serve by digging down through layers. Keeps for 4-5 days and never gets limp!
Serves:10-15 (Also for 2. It keeps so well you can eat "on it" for a week!

Favorite recipe of: Charles and Cynthia McGinnes
Career Highlights: Owners of Thornmar Farm in Chestertown, Maryland. With seven stallions, the McGinneses foal 95-100 mares every year.

"Furlong — One eight of a mile."

SPINACH SOUFFLE SALAD

1 small package lemon Jello
1 cup hot water
½ cup cold water
1 tablespoon vinegar
½ cup mayonnaise
½ teaspoon salt and pepper to taste
1 cup chopped fresh spinach
¾ cup cottage cheese
⅓ cup diced celery
1 tablespoon chopped fresh onion

Dissolve Jello in hot water, then beat with rotary beater. While beating, add cold water, vinegar, mayonnaise and seasonings. Blend until fluffy. Refrigerate 15-20 minutes or until lightly firm. Again, beat with rotary beater until fluffy. Fold in spinach, cottage cheese, celery and onion. Return to refrigerator until firm. This works well in a mold or 8x8-inch square pan.
Serves: 8

Origin: Mrs. Grady Roberts, Abilene, Texas
Favorite recipe of: Mrs. Louis (Nita) Brooks, Sweetwater, Texas
Racing interest: Thoroughbred owner and racing enthusiast.

JOCKEY JELLO DELIGHT

2 3-ounce packages orange or lime Jello (I prefer lime)
1 20-ounce can crushed pineapple
1 cup chopped walnuts, divided
1 small carton whipped topping
1 8-ounce package cream cheese, softened
1 tablespoon lemon juice
¾ cup sugar
2 tablespoons flour
2 eggs, beaten

Prepare Jello according to package directions. Chill until it begins to congeal. Drain pineapple, reserving juice. Add pineapple to Jello. Pour mixture into oiled 9x13-inch pan. Sprinkle with one-half of the walnuts. Chill until completely congealed. Blend whipped topping with cream cheese, and spread over congealed Jello. Cover and chill. Add enough water to pineapple juice to make one cup. In a saucepan combine lemon juice, sugar, flour, eggs and pineapple juice. Cook over low heat until thick; then chill thoroughly. When cool, spread over cream cheese. Sprinkle with remaining walnuts. Cut into squares and serve on a lettuce leaf.
Serves: 12-15

Origin: Mrs. Larry (Becky) Melancon
Favorite recipe of : Larry Melancon, Jockey, Louisville, Kentucky

"Jockey — Race rider; to maneuver for position during a race."

JOCKEY SALAD MEXICALI

4 cups chopped lettuce
1 16-ounce can frijole beans
2 medium tomatoes, chopped
1 4-ounce can chopped green chilies
1 medium avocado, ripe
½ cup sour cream
1 teaspoon chili powder
1 teaspoon instant minced onion
¼ teaspoon salt and pepper
½ cup shredded cheese
½ cup corn chips, crushed

Combine lettuce, drained beans, tomatoes and chilies in a salad bowl. Chill. Blend avocado and sour cream. Add chili powder, onion, salt and pepper and mix well. Toss salad with avocado dressing and top with cheese and chips.
Serves: 6

Origin: WIN-PLACE-SHOW RECIPES by Horsewomen United-
        Horsewomen United, Inc. is composed of female family members of owners, trainers, jockeys, and all track employees engaged in the state of New Mexico.
Favorite recipe of: Margaret Osborne duPont, El Paso, Texas
Career Highlights: United States National Tennis Champion 25 times (3 Women's Singles, 13 Women's Doubles, 9 Mixed Doubles - record still stands!); Wimbledon Women's Singles Champion 1947, Wimbledon Women's Doubles Champion 5 times, Wimbledon Mixed Doubles Champion 1962; Owner-breeder with Margaret Varner Bloss of filly *Net Effect*, 1984 winner Land of Enchantment Futurity; stakes winners *Half Smash* and *Tie Breaker*.

CHICKEN-FRUIT SALAD

3 cups chicken, cooked and cut in chunky pieces
¾ cup chopped celery
¾ cup red seedless grapes, halved
1 20-ounce can pineapple chunks in natural juice, drained
1 11-ounce can Mandarin oranges, drained
¼ cup pecans, chopped
¼ cup salad dressing
⅛ teaspoon salt
Lettuce leaves, as desired

Toss chicken, celery, grapes, pineapple, oranges and 3 tablespoons of the pecans together lightly. Gently mix salad dressing and salt with chicken mixture and chill. Serve on lettuce leaves. Garnish with remaining pecans. Calories per serving: about 225
Serves: 6

Origin: *The I Love America Diet* by Phyllis George and Bill Adler
Favorite recipe of: Phyllis George Brown
Career Highlights: Former First Lady of Kentucky as wife of Governor John Y. Brown; currently co-host of the CBS Morning News.

CONDITION BOOK CURRY

3 cups cooked turkey, cubed
1½ cups sliced celery
½ cup mayonnaise
¼ cup sour cream
1 teaspoon salt
⅛ teaspoon onion salt
Juice of 1 lemon
1-3 tablespoons curry powder, according to taste
Toasted almonds

Combine turkey with celery. Mix mayonnaise with sour cream, salt, onion salt, lemon juice and curry powder. Add mayonnaise mixture to turkey and celery. Serve on salad greens with sprinkling of toasted almonds.
Serves: 4

Origin: Mrs. Howard (Daisy) Battle
Favorite recipe of: Howard L. Battle, Racing Secretary, Keeneland Race Course
                Lexington, Kentucky

"Condition Book — Publication in which track announces purses, terms of eligibility and weight formulas of races."

ORANGE SALAD

1 pint sour cream
2 11-ounce cans Mandarin oranges, drained
1 20-ounce can chunk pineapple, drained
½ cup shredded coconut
1 6½-ounce package miniature marshmallows

Combine sour cream with drained oranges, pineapple and coconut. When mixture is well blended, add marshmallows. Refrigerate until ready to use. Easy salad for a pork roast! Also doubles as a dessert!
Serves: 8

Origin: Eileen Richard
Favorite recipe of: Don and Janet Stemmans
Racing interests: Owners of Stemmans, Inc., Carencro, Louisiana,
                 Tack specialists "For All Your Horse Needs"

RUTH BARKER'S HAWAIIAN SALAD

1 20-ounce can pineapple chunks
1 17-ounce can fruit cocktail
1 11-ounce can Mandarin oranges
1 3½-ounce package shredded coconut
1 6¼-ounce package miniature marshmallows
1 16-ounce carton sour cream
A few sliced Maraschino cherries

Drain pineapple, fruit cocktail and oranges in a colander. In a large mixing bowl, blend fruit with coconut, marshmallows and sour cream. Arrange cherries on top and refrigerate overnight. The refrigeration is necessary for the blending of all the ingredients.
Serves: 6-10

Origin: Ruth Barker of Norristown, Pennsylvania
Favorite recipe of: Salty Roberts, Cooper City, Florida
Career Highlights: Worked for some of the finest trainers including: Ben and Jimmy
                 Jones, Preston Birch, E. I. Kelly, Woody Stephens and Bennie
                 Stutts. Galloped such good horses as *Armed, Greek Ship, Sun Glow,*
                 Blue Hills, Chains and probably one of the greatest, *Sir Mango* who
                 won eight straight stake races. Greatest highlight during 36 plus
                 years on the track was establishing the Race Track Chaplaincy
                 of America and the Race Track Chaplaincy of California to bring the
                 love of God to folks on the backside. We minister to the needs of the
                 total man; spiritual, physical and social.

PASTA SALAD ANTHONY

1 8-ounce package shell macaroni
1 can rinsed garbanzo beans
1 can tuna in spring water
1 small purple onion, chopped
⅓ cup chopped parsley
1 clove garlic, minced
1 small bottle stuffed olives, chopped plus a little juice
⅓ cup lemon juice
1 tablespoon Dijon mustard
¾-1 cup mayonnaise

Cook macaroni according to package directions and drain well. Add beans, tuna and all chopped ingredients and toss lightly. Make sauce combining mayonnaise, mustard and lemon juice. Pour over pasta mix and refrigerate overnight.
Variations: May use shrimp, crabmeat or chicken instead of tuna.
Serves: 6

Origin: Mrs. John Ed (Mary Lynn) Anthony
Favorite recipe of: John Ed Anthony, Fordyce, Arkansas
Career Highlight: Owned *Cox's Ridge*, 1980 Eclipse Award winner as Champion
          3-year-old colt.

QUARTER POLE PASTA SALAD

1 pound spaghetti
1 red onion, chopped fine
6 green onions, chopped fine
1 cucumber, chopped fine
3 ripe tomatoes, chopped fine
½ cup dried mixed salad seasonings
¾ bottle Italian dressing

Break spaghetti into three sections and cook as directed. Drain. Toss all ingredients with spaghetti. Refrigerate overnight.
Serves: 8

Origin: Mrs. Julio (Kim) Espinoza
Favorite recipe of: Julio Espinoza, Louisville, Kentucky
Career Highlights: Rider of the winner of the Phoenix Handicap, the oldest stake
          race in the country, four times in a row at Keeneland Race Course.

"Quarter pole — Colored post at infield rail exactly two furlongs from finish wire."

CRABMEAT SALAD

1 8-ounce package cream cheese
½ cup butter
1 pound white crabmeat
1 small finely chopped onion
1 teaspoon Tabasco sauce
1 teaspoon finely minced garlic
Red pepper to taste
6 large California avocados, cut in half lengthwise and peeled

In double boiler, melt cream cheese and butter. Add crabmeat and all other ingredients. Stir until well blended. Place peeled avocados on lettuce leaves and a scoop of crabmeat mixture on top of each half. Garnish with fresh parsley and lemon wedges.
Serves: 6

Origin: Pamela J. Fitzgerald
Favorite recipe of: Frank L. Brothers, Trainer, Shreveport, Louisiana
Career Highlights: Won Louisiana Downs training title five straight seasons (1980-1984); ranked fifth nationally with 158 wins in 1984; all-time leading stakes winner with a record 64 career wins at the end of the 1984 season; trained three of Louisiana Downs' top 10 money winners, *Dramatic Desire, Coast Patrol* and *Temerity Prince,* in 1984 and five of the track's top 20.

TRIPLE CROWN CRAB LOUIS

2 heads Boston lettuce
1 pound crab meat
4 hard boiled eggs, quartered
4 tomtaoes, quartered
1 cup mayonnaise
½ cup heavy cream, whipped
½ cup chili sauce
¼ cup chopped green pepper
¼ cup chopped green onion tops

Clean and separate lettuce leaves and chill. On a large platter or on individual serving dishes, arrange lettuce with crab meat in the center. Arrange eggs and tomatoes around crab meat. Mix the remaining ingredients to make the dressing and spoon over top of salad.
Serves: 4-8

Favorite recipe of: Joe King, Trainer, Louisville, Kentucky

"Triple Crown — Mythical award to any three-year-old that wins the Kentucky Derby, Preakness Stakes and Belmont Stakes."

OL' TOM'S BLEU CHEESE DRESSING

4 ounces bleu cheese
¼ cup condensed milk
¼ cup mayonnaise
Worcestershire to taste
1 tablespoon lemon juice
Dash of black pepper
Sprinkle of parsley, ¼ teaspoon

Crumble cheese and mix well with other ingredients. Let sit in refrigerator for 2 days, then gain weight!
Yield: 8 ounces

Favorite recipe of: Tom Russell, Red Oak, Texas
Career Highlights: Sales Coordinator of Hits Parade Sale; founder of the Horsemen's Credit Union; President of Texas Thoroughbred Breeders Association; President of Texas Breeders Association.

SPINACH SALAD DRESSING

1½ tablespoons minced green onions
3 tablespoons Dijon mustard
1⅓ tablespoons Accent
1⅓ tablespoons salt
⅔ cup vinegar
⅔ cup warm water
1 tablespoon Worcestershire sauce
1 dash Tabasco sauce
½ cup olive oil
½ cup salad oil

Place onions, mustard, Accent, salt, vinegar and water in blender and blend for 30 seconds. Gradually stir in remaining ingredients and mix well. Pour over spinach leaves, sliced mushrooms, croutons, crumbled bacon and sliced hard boiled eggs. Keeps well in refrigerator.
Yield: About 2½ cups

Origin: Houlihan's Restaurant in New Orleans, Louisiana
Favorite recipe of: Joe Ferrer, Jockey Agent, New Orleans, Louisiana

And They're Off

Meats

Poultry

Seafood

Wild Game

STEAK WITH WHISKEY SAUCE

Marinate steak for 15 minutes on each side with a mixture of:
½ Whiskey
½ Soy sauce

Sprinkle steak with garlic salt and broil or barbeque as you prefer.

Favorite recipe of: Robert Holthus, Hot Springs, Arkansas
Career Highlights: Leading trainer at Oaklawn Park six times (1967, 1971, 1977, 1978, 1982 & 1985); won titles at Arlington Park, Hawthorne and Detroit.

BLACK TYPE STROGANOFF

2 pounds sirloin, sliced into ½-inch strips
4 tablespoons butter
1 cup chopped onion
1 clove garlic, finely chopped
3 tablespoons flour
1 teaspoon meat extract paste, optional
1 tablespoon ketchup
½ teaspoon salt
⅛ teaspoon pepper
1 10½-ounce can beef bouillon, undiluted
¼ teaspoon dried dill
1 10½-ounce can cream of mushroom or cream of chicken soup
½ cup sour cream
1 6-ounce can sliced mushrooms, drained

Heat large skillet. Melt 1 tablespoon butter. Sear meat quickly on all sides. Remove from skillet. Saute onion and garlic in 3 tablespoons hot butter until golden. Remove from heat. Add flour, meat-extract paste, ketchup, salt and pepper and stir until smooth. Gradually add bouillon and bring to boil, stirring. Simmer 5 minutes. Over low heat, add dill, soup and sour cream. Stir until combined. Add mushrooms and beef; simmer slowly just until sauce and beef are hot. Serve with rice. Sprinkle with parsley.
Serves: 4-5

Origin: Mrs. Howard L. (Daisy) Battle
Favorite recipe of: Howard L. Battle, Racing Secretary, Keeneland Race Course
                    Lexington, Kentucky

"Clocker — Person who times workouts, usually for betting information."

DOC SEVERINSEN'S BRACIOLA

1 full cut beef bottom round (2-2½ pounds) cut ½ inch thick
Salt and freshly ground black pepper
¼ pound prosciutto or more to taste, minced
½ cup chopped fresh parsley
2 hard cooked eggs, chopped
2 small cloves garlic, minced
¼ cup freshly grated Parmesan cheese or to taste
⅓ cup raisins, soaked in small amount of water to plump or
        1 small carrot, grated
⅓ cup pine nuts
Handful fine bread crumbs (optional)
2 tablespoons cooking oil or 1 tablespoon each butter and cooking oil
1 stalk celery, chopped
¼ cup chopped onion
⅓ cup dry red wine
1 can (16 ounces) Italian plum tomatoes
½ teaspoon Italian seasoning

Flatten meat with mallet to ¼ inch thickness. Season both sides with salt and pepper. Combine prosciutto, parsley, eggs, half of minced garlic, ½ cup cheese, raisins or half of grated carrot, pine nuts and bread crumbs. Spread stuffing evenly over meat. Starting at narrow end, roll steak jellyroll fashion. Tie with string at 1-inch intervals or fasten with toothpicks.
Heat oil in large skillet. Brown meat well on all sides, remove to platter. Saute remaining garlic and carrot, celery and onion until wilted; remove to platter.
Drain off excess fat. Add wine to skillet to deglaze pan drippings. Return meat and vegetables to skillet with remaining ¼ cup cheese, undrained tomatoes and Italian seasoning. Meat should be covered with vegetables and tomatoes. If not, add small amount of water to cover. Cover tightly. Simmer about 1 hour.
Remove meat, strain sauce, cool and remove any fat that comes to surface. Return meat and sauce to skillet; continue cooking, covered until meat is tender. Remove string from meat, slice and serve with sauce and spaghetti if desired.
Serves: 4-6

Favorite recipe of: Doc Severinsen, Tonight Show, Burbank, California
Racing interest: Thoroughbred owner and racing enthusiast

BURT'S BEEF STEW

3 slices bacon, cut in small pieces
4 tablespoons flour
1 teaspoon salt
½ teaspoon pepper
2 pounds lean beef (chuck is juicy) cut in 1-inch pieces
1 large onion, chopped (1 cup)
1 clove garlic, minced
1 can tomato sauce (8-ounces)
½ can condensed beef broth
1 cup good, dry burgundy wine
1 bay leaf, if you like it
1 pinch thyme
2 carrots, cut up coarsely (1 cup)
2 stalks celery, cut up coarsely (¾ cup)
2 potatoes, pared and quartered
6-8 fresh mushrooms, sliced

Cook bacon until crisp in a large, heavy pot. Combine flour, salt and pepper; dip beef in flour mixture to coat completely. Brown in bacon fat, turning often. (Add a little vegetable oil if needed.) Add onion, garlic and brown a little. Add tomato sauce, broth, wine, bay leaf and thyme. Cover and cook slowly for about 1½ hours. Add carrots, celery, then potatoes and mushrooms. Uncover and cook until meat and vegetables are tender.
Serves: 4

Favorite recipe of: Burt Reynolds, Actor, Burbank, California
Racing interests: Thoroughbred owner and racing enthusiast.

SEATTLE STEW

2 pounds stewing beef, cubed
5 medium potatoes, quartered
6 carrots, sliced thick
2 medium onions, sliced
1 5-ounce can mushrooms
3 tablespoons minute tapioca
1 18-ounce can mixed vegetable juice

Place meat and vegetables together in Dutch oven or slow cooker. Mix tapioca with a small amount of juice and pour over vegetable mixture. Pour remaining juice over all. Cover and cook in 300° oven for five hours; or slow cooker for six hours. DO NOT PEEK.
Serves: 6

Origin: Mrs. Joe (Terry) King's aunt.
Favorite recipe of: Joe King, Trainer, Louisville, Kentucky

"*Seattle Slew* — 1977 winner of the Triple Crown."

FISHERMAN'S POT ROAST

Beef chuck or shoulder roast
1 small bottle ketchup
2 tablespoons butter
¼ teaspoon oregano, optional
1 large diced onion
1 tablespoon vinegar
1 teaspoon Worcestershire sauce
Salt, to taste
Pepper, to taste

Combine all ingredients except roast in a saucepan over low heat and stir until well blended. Pour over browned roast in a heavy roasting pan. Simmer about 2 hours, depending on size of roast. Add potatoes and carrots and simmer an additional 30 minutes or until vegetables are tender.
Serves: 6-8

Origin: Archie Lofton, Wichita Falls, Texas
Racing interest: Thoroughbred owner and racing enthusiast

GENE'S POST TIME STEW

4-5 pounds lean stew meat, seasoned
4 large bell peppers, chopped
Celery to taste, chopped
4 large onions, chopped fine
3-4 large cans stewed tomatoes, or whole tomatoes
2 bunches carrots, cleaned and sliced
5-6 large potatoes, cubed
Small package noodles (8-ounce)
Salt, garlic salt, Accent, pepper and sugar, to taste

Brown meat, onions, celery and peppers slightly, Add water and let simmer until mixed. Add all vegetables. DO NOT ADD NOODLES UNTIL JUST ABOUT COOKED. Add enough water to adequately cover and season to suit taste. Cover partially and simmer on medium heat until thick and flavorful. Add noodles about an hour before serving.
Serves: 14-30, depending on eaters.

Origin: Developed by Gene Norman for those cold winter days at the Fair Grounds.
Favorite recipe of: Gene Norman, Trainer, Bossier City, Louisiana
Career Highlights: Trainer of the Year, 1983, HBPA Banquet Awards; HBPA Board Member, 3 years, Vice President, 1 term; Trainer for 20 years, winner of various stakes with *Dr. Box, Worthy Melody, Lil Liza Jane, Boldansexy* and *Explosive Wagon;* Ran in Kentucky Derby and Super Derby in 1983 with *Explosive Wagon;* Co-ordinator of Louisiana Race Track Chaplaincy; married to Revella and dad of Cody and Cole Norman.

"Post Time — When horses enter the starting gate."

CHINESE BOOKIE
(Orange Peel Beef)

12-ounce flank steak, cut in strips 2 inches wide, ¼ inch thick
1 teaspoon baking soda
2 tablespoons corn starch
½ teaspoon salt
½ teaspoon MSG
Pinch black pepper
¼ cup + 2 tablespoons cooking oil
1 green onion, chopped
1 teaspoon ginger
2 cloves garlic, finely chopped
Peel of ½ orange which has been dried for 24 hours, sliced thin
1 teaspoon soy sauce
1 tablespoon sugar
Dried red peppers, to taste (optional)
1 tablespoon oyster sauce (optional)
Cooked rice

Marinate flank steak for at least 2 hours in a mixture of baking soda, cornstarch, salt, MSG, black pepper and 2 tablespoons water. Just before cooking, add ¼ cup oil. Have wok or skillet very hot (450°). Remove steak from marinate and place in wok for 2 minutes stirring and turning frequently. Remove and clean wok, turn heat down to 350° which is not quite smoking. Add 2 tablespoons fresh oil and stir fry green onion, ginger, garlic, orange peel and dried red peppers if desired for 2½ minutes. Add beef to vegetables for 3 or 4 stirs, then add soy sauce, sugar, oyster sauce and stir 3 or 4 more times. Serve over rice.
Serves: 2, may be doubled or increased to any amount.

Origin: Wong Hun Lo, a Bookie in California.
Favorite recipe of: Rae Johnson, Hot Springs, Arkansas
Career Highlights: Former Thoroughbred owner and retired pony girl who has taken three Kentucky Derby winners to the post. Owner of Jockey Club Gift Shop in Hot Springs, Arkansas.

"Bookie — Bookmaker, one who accepts and pays off bets."

SPANISH ROUND STEAK

2 pounds beef round steak, cut ¾-inch thick
⅓ cup flour (seasoned with salt and pepper)
¼ cup oil
1 teaspoon cumin
1 teaspoon sugar
28-ounce can tomatoes, drained and chopped (reserve liquid)
2 tablespoons lemon juice
1 garlic clove, crushed
1 beef bouillon cube, dissolved in ½ cup boiling water
1 green pepper, chopped
1 onion, chopped
4-ounce can green chilies
⅓ cup fresh parsley, chopped
⅓ cup raisins

Cut steak into ¼-inch strips. (this will be easy to cut if steak is partially frozen). Dredge strips in flour and in a saucepan brown on all sides in the oil. Pour off drippings and sprinkle meat with cumin and sugar. Add tomato liquid and the next eight ingredients. Stir until well blended and simmer, covered, for 45 minutes, stirring occasionally. Stir in the tomatoes and simmer, covered, for 15 minutes or longer, until meat is tender. Serve over rice.
    "A favorite in the Sweetwater area. Good left over or frozen!"
Serves: 8

Origin: *Under the Mushroom* Cookbook
Favorite recipe of: Mrs. Louis (Nita) Brooks, Sweetwater, Texas
Racing interest: Thoroughbred owner and racing enthusiast.

BACKSIDE BRISKET

3-4 pound brisket roast
Liquid smoke
Garlic salt
Celery salt
Onion salt
Worcestershire sauce
Black pepper
Barbecue sauce, optional

Pour liquid smoke on both sides of roast, then sprinkle with garlic, celery and onion salt. Cover and refrigerate overnight. Before cooking, pour Worcestershire sauce on both sides and sprinkle with pepper and additional salt if desired. Cook for six hours at 275°. You may pour barbecue sauce over the brisket 1 hour before end of cooking time if desired.
Serves: 8-10

Origin: Mrs. Don (Roylynn) Von Hemel
Favorite recipe of: Don Von Hemel, Trainer, Omaha, Nebraska

ROAST BEEF WITH YORKSHIRE PUDDING

1 5-pound standing rib or rib eye roast
Seasoning according to taste
2 eggs, beaten
1 cup flour, sifted
1 cup milk
½ teaspoon salt

Season roast according to taste and cook at 350° for approximately 2-2½ hours. This will be medium to well. Shorten cooking time for rareness. Prepare Yorkshire ahead preferably in afternoon so that you can refrigerate for an hour or so before cooking.
Mix eggs with flour and gradually add milk. Mix to the consistency of pancake batter. Add salt and refrigerate, covered for 1-1½ hours. About ½ hour before roast is done, increase temperature to 400°. Remove meat to a platter, cover with foil and keep warm on top of stove. Remove some of the suet or fat from the meat drippings and put about one tablespoon in 12 cupcake tins. Place cupcake pan in oven for suet to get hot. Remove Yorkshire from refrigerator and beat well adding a drop of water. When suet is sizzling, pour batter into cupcake tins, ½ full. Cook on top rack of oven for about 35 minutes, until brown. Should be hollow inside. Makes about 12 popovers. Serve with roast and beef gravy.
Serves: 6

Origin: Yorkshire, England
Favorite recipe of: Terrance Dunlavy, Hot Springs, Arkansas
Career Highlights: A former jockey, born in Kent, England, who had the mount aboard Narushua in the 1965 Kentucky Derby, Terry is a respected trainer on the Louisiana-Arkansas circuit. In 1981 ran *Dr. Spanky* in the Super Derby and finished fifth with some of the better three year olds.

TAP CITY PARMIGIANA

6 minute steaks
1 beaten egg and dash pepper
⅓ cup grated Parmesan cheese
⅓ cup fine dry bread crumbs
⅓ cup Wesson oil
1 8-ounce jar pizza sauce
½ pound mozzarella cheese, sliced or shredded

Dip steaks in egg and pepper; roll in mixture of Parmesan cheese and bread crumbs. Brown well on both sides in oil. Place flat in greased baking dish. Top each piece with pizza sauce, then cheese and add more pizza sauce. Can sprinkle with Parmesan cheese if desired. Bake at 325° for about 20 minutes. Can be prepared early and baked later.
Serves: 6

Origin: "A Daisy creation"
Favorite recipe of: Howard L. Battle, Racing Secretary, Keeneland Race Course
                Lexington, Kentucky

SHOEMAKER'S CHILI CASSEROLE

1 tablespoon butter or margarine
1¼ cup chopped onion
¼ cup chopped pimento
1 tablespoon chopped mild green chilies
2 tablespoons chopped scallions
4 cups corn chips, coarsely crushed
2 cans chili con carne with beans
2 cups shredded Cheddar cheese

Preheat oven to 400°. Grease a 1½-quart baking dish with butter or margarine. Saute onion in butter until transparent. Remove from heat and stir in pimento, chilies and scallions. Line the bottom of the baking dish with crushed corn chips. Carefully spread half of the chili con carne over the chips. Layer half of the onion mixture and 1½ cups of shredded cheese. Repeat chili, onion mixture layers. Sprinkle with remaining ½ cup of cheese on top of casserole. Bake 20-25 minutes.
Note from Cindy Shoemaker: If you want to spice it up, use Jalapeno peppers instead of the green chilies, or chili con carne with beans (hot), but I don't recommend using both!
Serves: 6-8

Favorite recipe of: William Shoemaker, Jockey, San Marino, California
Career Highlights: Led the United States in money won a record of seven consecutive years in the late 1950's and early 1960's. Record of riding 485 winners in one year stood for 17 years. Won the Kentucky Derby three times, the Belmont Stakes five times, and the Preakness twice, riding horses such as *Swaps, Round Table, Forego, Gallant Man, Northern Dancer, Gun Bow, Damascus, Cougar II, Ack Ack* and *Exceller.*

GONE BROKE GOULASH

2 pounds ground beef
1 medium sized onion, chopped
1 green pepper, chopped
Garlic salt to taste
1 8-ounce package noodles
1 8-ounce can tomato sauce
¼ cup ketchup

Brown the beef along with onion, pepper and added garlic salt. Boil noodles separately. After adding them to ground beef, add tomato sauce and allow to simmer for 20 minutes. Add ketchup. "Best served with peanut-buttered white bread and a chilled Dr. Pepper. This recipe was developed years ago after an incredible cold streak of betting that involved the loss of 19 straight photo finishes." John McEvoy
Serves: Depends upon cold (or hot) streak.

Origin: Florence Trainor, an inveterate bettor. (McEvoy's aunt)
Favorite recipe of: John McEvoy, Chicago, Illinois
Career Highlights: Editor, Midwest Edition of Daily Racing Form.

STOOPER'S STEW

2 pounds stew meat
1 tablespoon mustard
1 tablespoon ketchup
¼ cup sherry
1 package brown gravy mix
1 16-ounce can vegetables, drained
Prepared rice or noodles

In a crockpot add trimmed stew meat and cover with mustard, ketchup, sherry and gravy mix. Add your favorite vegetable, (Mel prefers green beans) and let cook on low for 8-10 hours. Serve over rice or noodles.
Serves: 4

Origin: World's Poorest Stooper
Favorite recipe of: Mel Chadwell, Director of Racing and Racing Secretary,
　　　　　　Tampa Bay Downs, Oldsmar, Florida
Career Highlights:　Racing Secretary at Thistledown for 7 years until 1980, Racing
　　　　　　Secretary or Steward at River Downs, Darby Downs, Commodore,
　　　　　　Arapahoe and Tampa Bay Downs.

GRANDMA'S GOULASH

¾ 16-ounce package spaghetti
1 pound ground round
½ onion, chopped
1 8-ounce can tomato sauce
1 can creamed corn
1 can olives, pitted and sliced or chopped

Prepare spaghetti according to package directions. Brown ground round with chopped onions and drain. Add to cooked spaghetti: beef, tomato sauce, creamed corn and olives. Mix well and put in 9x13-inch baking dish. Heat until bubbling at 350°, about 30 minutes. Freezes well.
Serves: 4-6

Origin: Mike Spencer's Grandmother
Favorite recipe of: Mike Spencer, Kersey, Colorado
Career Highlights:　Chaplain at Oaklawn Park, Hot Springs, Arkansas; Professional
　　　　　　Rodeo Clown.

"Stooper — One of several dozen Americans who make a precarious living by picking up discarded mutuel tickets at tracks and cashing those that have been thrown away by mistake."

MEL'S CHILI

2 pounds lean ground beef
1 onion, chopped
2 cans tomato paste
6 cans water
1 clove garlic, mashed
Salt and pepper
1 large can chili beans
2 packages chili seasoning mix

Brown meat, add onions and saute until tender. Stir in tomato paste, water, garlic. Simmer until thick, about two hours. Add remaining ingredients and cook about 15 minutes longer. Serve as is, or it is delicious over spaghetti and topped with cheese.
Serves: 8-10

Favorite recipe of: Vic Tayback, Actor "Mel" on TV's "Alice" Los Angeles, California
Racing interests: Thoroughbred owner and racing enthusiast.

STRETCH DRIVE CHILI

2 pounds ground round beef
2 large onions, chopped
4 green peppers, chopped
Salt and pepper, to taste
2 16-ounce cans tomatoes
4 16-ounce cans kidney beans
3 tablespoons chili powder

In a large pan, brown the ground beef. Add onions, green peppers, salt and pepper and cook over medium heat for 20 minutes. Add tomatoes, chili powder and beans. Cook over low heat for 1 hour. Chili can be made ahead of time and reheated, in fact it's better if you do so.
Serves: 8-10

Favorite recipe of: J. WIlliam Boniface, Bonita Farm, Darlington, Maryland
Career Highlights: Trained and owned the 1983 Preakness winner,
Deputed Testamony.

"Dead Heat — When two or more horses reach finish wire simultaneously."

LASAGNE

2 cups minced onions
8 cloves minced garlic
2 pounds ground beef
1 large can tomato puree
2 large cans tomato paste
1 teaspoon oregano
1½ tablespoons salt
1 teaspoon dry basil
¼ teaspoon pepper
2 pounds lasagne noodles
2½ quarts boiling water
2 cups ricotta cheese
1 pounds sliced mozzarella cheese
1 cup grated Romano cheese

Saute onions, garlic and meat in 1 tablespoon shortening over medium heat until redness disappears. Add tomato puree, tomato paste, oregano, salt, basil and pepper. Simmer and stir occasionally for 1 hour. In meantime, cook lasagne noodles in water with about 1 tablespoon salt for 15-20 minutes. Drain. Pour ⅓ hot tomato-meat sauce in large lasagne dish. Layer noodles over sauce, ½ ricotta cheese, ⅓ mozzarella slices and ½ Romano cheese. Repeat layers as above, ending with remaining sauce and mozzarella cheese slices on top. Bake at 350° for 20 minutes or until bubbly.
Serves: 12

Origin: Mervin's Mother, Mrs. Frances Muniz
Favorite recipe of: Mervin Muniz Jr., Racing Secretary, Fair Grounds,
                New Orleans, Louisiana
Career Highlights: Racing Secretary at the Fair Grounds since 1977; State Steward
                in Ohio at Thistle Downs Race Track since 1983. Director of
                Racing at Evangeline Downs in 1985, prior to that, Racing Secretary
                at Evangeline Downs since 1974; Racing Secretary at Jefferson
                Downs in 1972-73; Racing Secretary at Scarborough Downs in
                Maine; Racing Secretary at River Downs; Paddock Judge
                at Suffolk Downs in Massachusetts.

"Stewards — The three duly-appointed arbiters of racing law who judge human and equine conduct at a race meeting."

FRED STONE'S STUFFED CABBAGE

2 heads cabbage
1 onion
2 pounds lean ground beef
2 eggs
1 cup rice, uncooked
Salt, to taste
Garlic or garlic powder, to taste
Large can of tomatoes
8-ounce can tomato sauce
6-ounce can tomato puree
Water
1 cup sugar
Sour salt

Remove leaves from cabbage heads and pack loosely in large pot. Steam in hot water until leaves are soft. Mix beef, eggs, rice, salt and crushed garlic or powder. Roll small amount of beef mixture into each cabbage leaf. Poke in ends and rolls will not unravel. Slice remaining cabbage and onion and place in roasting pan. Arrange cabbage rolls on top. Add cans of tomatoes, sauce and puree. Add sugar, more salt and pour sour salt crystals into your hand to measure about the size of a nickel. Add water to almost cover. Bake at 325°, covered, for about 6 to 8 hours. Add more water if needed. Taste and add more seasoning if needed. This recipe can be prepared in advance and is even better when you do so.
Serves: 8

Favorite recipe of: Fred Stone, Equine Artist, Agoura, California
Career Highlights: Fred Stone lists his most famous works:
  "The Shoe — 8,000 Wins", "The Eternal Legacy" and
  "The Final Thunder — Man O' War" and a book to be released in
  October, 1985, *FRED STONE PAINS THE SPORT OF KINGS.*

"This recipe is like the concoctions that trainers put on their horses legs. It is your own personal touch that makes it better!"

Actor Jack Klugman with friend, *Jacklin Klugman*,
who ran third in the 1980 Kentucky Derby.

JACK KLUGMAN'S
SPAGHETTI SAUCE RECIPE

⅓ cup olive oil
3 pounds pork with bone
1 pound sweet sausage
1 pound hot sausage
3 32-ounce cans whole tomatoes
2 16-ounce cans tomato puree
⅔ can water (whole tomato sized can)
1 6-ounce can tomato paste
1 6-ounce can water
14 cloves garlic, pressed
To taste: salt, pepper, fresh oregano, basil leaves, parsley

Heat oil, add garlic and brown. Add pork, sweet sausage and hot sausage and brown. Put whole tomatoes, tomato puree, tomato paste and all water in blender; blend well. Add this tomato mixture and seasonings to meat and garlic while stirring. Bring to a boil and place lid on and simmer for 2 hours, consistently stirring at least every 15 minutes.
Serves: A Crowd

Favorite recipe of: Jack Klugman, Actor, Universal City, California
Racing interest: Thoroughbred owner and racing enthusiast

CREOLE JAMBALAYA

1 pound smoked sausage, sliced
1 cup chopped green pepper
1 cup chopped onion
1 clove garlic, crushed
1 tablespoon all purpose flour
1 28-ounce can tomatoes, undrained
2½ cups water
2 tablespoons chopped, fresh parsley
2 cups uncooked white rice
2 tablespoons Worcestershire sauce
2 teaspoons salt
½ teaspoon dried whole thyme
¼ teaspoon red pepper
1½ pound shrimp, peeled and deveined

Cook sausage until browned in a large dutch oven. Drain off all but 2 tablespoons pan drippings. Add green pepper, onion and garlic; cook until vegetables are tender. Add flour and stir until well blended. Stir in tomatoes, water and parsley; bring to a boil. Add remaining ingredients except shrimp; return to a boil. Reduce heat and simmer, covered, 20 minutes. Add shrimp; cover and cook an additional 10 minutes.
Serves: 10

Origin: Katherine Von Gohren, Metairie, Louisiana
Favorite recipe of: The Editor

BRENDA'S LUCKY SPAGHETTI SAUCE

2½ pounds extra lean ground beef
1 large onion, chopped
4 large stalks celery, chopped
2 tablespoons vegetable oil
1 9-ounce can sliced mushrooms or ½ pound fresh mushrooms, sliced
1½ jars 32-ounce spaghetti sauce
½ can tomato soup
3 ounces tomato paste
1 cup water
Pepper
Oregano

Brown ground meat in a heavy skillet; drain well. Saute onion and celery in oil, then add to ground meat. (If using fresh mushrooms, saute with other vegetables.) Add mushrooms, spaghetti sauce, tomato soup, tomato paste, water and stir well. Add pepper and oregano to taste. Simmer uncovered over very low heat for one hour.
Serves: 10

Favorite recipe of: Brenda Wilson, Trainer, Cicero, Illinois

SAUSAGE CASSEROLE

2 pounds bulk sausage, 1½ pounds regular and ½ pound hot
2 tablespoons margarine
3 cups chopped celery
2 cups chopped onion
1 green pepper, chopped
8 cups water
4 envelopes dry chicken noodle soup mix
1 cup raw rice
1 cup slivered almonds or 1 can water chestnuts, sliced thinly

Cook sausage and drain well. Saute vegetables in margarine. Combine water, soup mix and rice. Cook slowly until all water is absorbed. Mixture will be wet, but no visible water. Mix all ingredients. Fold in almonds or water chestnuts. Pour into 9x13-inch pan. Bake covered for 40 minutes and uncovered 20 additional minutes in 350° oven.
Serves: 8

Origin: Mrs. John (Alta) Franks
Favorite recipe of: John Franks, Shreveport, Louisiana
Career Highlights: Honored for two consecutive years (1983-1984) as racing's outstanding owner.

BEEF AND SAUSAGE CASSEROLE

24 link sausages
½ pound fresh mushrooms, sliced
2 medium tomatoes, peeled, seeded and chopped
1 green pepper, seeded and chopped
1 medium onion, chopped
1 pound ground beef
1 tablespoon anchovy paste, optional
½ teaspoon dry mustard
⅛ teaspoon cayenne pepper
2 tablespoons dry sherry
1 10½-ounce can cream of mushroom soup
1 package canned biscuits, 10-count

In a large frying pan, fry sausage until well browned and cooked through. Remove from pan and drain on paper towels. Reserve 2 tablespoons drippings and discard the rest. In reserved drippings, saute the mushrooms, tomatoes, pepper and onion for about 10 minutes or until most of the liquid has cooked away. Add meat and brown. Be sure to drain off any grease after browning beef. Add anchovy paste, cayenne, mustard, sherry and soup and simmer for 15 minutes. Heat oven to 375°. Arrange 12 sausages on bottom of a shallow 3-quart casserole. Pour in beef mixture and top with remaining 12 sausages. Drop biscuits between sausage links. Bake uncovered 15 to 20 minutes or until mixture is heated through and biscuits are brown.
Serves: 6-8

Favorite recipe of: Joseph W. Harper, Del Mar, California
Career Highlights: Executive Vice President and General Manager, Del Mar
Thoroughbred Club; Member of the Jockey Club; past President,
Federation of California Racing Associations; Thoroughbred
owner and breeder; Member of Board of Directors,
Southern California Equine Foundation.

ECLIPSE AWARD WINNING RIBS

4-5 racks baby pork back ribs
1 cup brown sugar
1 cup ketchup
½ cup vinegar, or to taste
¼ cup Worcestershire sauce
¼ cup soy sauce
1 onion, chopped
Pinch salt and pepper
Garlic powder, to taste
1 tablespoon lemon juice

Mix all ingredients except ribs to make a sauce. Marinate ribs in sauce and cover with foil for 4-5 hours. (This is the secret — don't scrimp on time!) Bake in a roasting pan with cover for 1½-2 hours at 350°. Check ribs after 1½ hours; if they are close to being white in center, take out and place on hot barbecue grill. Cook while turning and brushing with sauce until they brown nicely. And VIOLA!!
Serves: 8

Origin: Jockey Leroy Moyers and Beverly Moyers
Favorite recipe of: Chris McCarron, Jockey, Glendale, California
Career Highlights: In 1974, as an apprentice, broke world record for number of wins, 546, previously 515; in 1980, leading rider in United States in races and money won; in 1981, broke record for money won, over $8 million. Eclipse Award in 1984 for leading rider in money won.

SALTY DOG'S RIBS

8 slabs baby pork ribs (2½ pounds per slab)
1 32-ounce jar honey
5 18-ounce bottles barbecue sauce
2 lined 16x10x2½-inch pans, lined with heavy duty foil

Use enough foil on sides of pan so that you can completely cover contents. Also saves on clean-up.

Trim all excess fat from outside of ribs. Separate short back rib from main rib; then separate ribs from each other in two's.

Have large pot of boiling, salted water ready. Place ribs in water for about 10 minutes until all redness is gone. Be careful not to over boil as the meat will fall off the bones.

Remove ribs to a colander to drain until you can handle them. They should be quite warm. Coat each rib liberally with honey using a small paint brush. Ribs must be hot in order for honey to be absorbed.

Pour one bottle of barbecue sauce over bottom of each pan. Place ribs in an orderly fashion in pans and coat completely with another bottle of sauce.

Use excess foil and cover ribs completely. Place in preheated 350° oven and allow to bake for 1 hour.

Remove from oven and baste with remaining sauce. Return to oven uncovered and bake for another hour basting and turning frequently.
Serves: 10-12

Favorite recipe of: W. H. "Salty" Roberts, Cooper City, Florida
Career Highlights: Worked for some of the finest trainers, including
Ben and Jimmy Jones, Preston Birch, E. I. Kelly, Woody
Stephens and Bennie Stutts. Galloped such good horses as *Armed,
Greek Ship, Sun Glow, Blue Hills, Chains* and probably
one of the greatest, *Sir Mango* who won eight
straight stakes.
Established the Race Track Chaplaincy of America and the
Race Track Chaplaincy of California to bring the love of
God to folks on the backside. "We minister to the needs of the
total man — spiritual, physical and social."

TODAY'S PICK —
PORK CHOPS & RICE

6 pork chops
Salt and pepper
1½ tablespoons vegetable oil
1 large bell pepper, sliced
1 large onion, sliced
1 16-ounce can tomatoes
1 cup chicken broth
1 cup rice, uncooked
1½ teaspoons salt
½ teaspoon oregano
½ teaspoon basil
¼ teaspoon pepper
¼ teaspoon garlic powder
1 teaspoon sugar

Season chops with salt and pepper to taste. Brown chops on both sides in vegetable oil in a large skillet. Remove chops from skillet and set aside. Put onions and pepper in skillet and saute until tender. Add rest of ingredients and bring to a boil. Arrange chops on top and simmer covered for 30 minutes.
Serves: 6

Favorite recipe of: Lela Willoughby, Robstown, Texas
Racing interest: Thoroughbred owner and racing enthusiast.

VEAL CORDON BLEU

*4 boneless veal cutlets, about 4 ounces each
4 thin slices boiled ham
4 thin slices Swiss cheese
2 tablespoons flour
½ teaspoon salt
¼ teaspoon pepper
¼ teaspoon allspice
1 egg, slightly beaten
½ cup dry bread crumbs
3 tablespoons vegetable oil
2 tablespoons water

Pound meat until ¼ inch thick. Place a slice of cheese, then a slice of ham on each cutlet. Roll up carefully, beginning at narrow end; secure rolls with wooden picks. Mix flour, salt, pepper and allspice; coat rolls with flour mixture. Dip rolls into egg, then roll in bread crumbs. In a large skillet, brown rolls in oil, about five minutes. Reduce heat and add water. Cover; simmer 45 minutes or until tender. Remove cover last 2-3 minutes to crisp rolls slightly. Serve over buttered noodles or fettuccine.
Substitution: Chicken breasts may be substituted for veal cutlets.
Serves: 4

Favorite recipe of: The Editor

CREOLE-ACADIAN VEAL STEW

4 pounds lean boneless veal shoulder, cut into 1½-inch cubes
2 teaspoons salt
¼ teaspoon fresh ground pepper
½ cup flour
4 tablespoons butter
¼-½ cup vegetable oil
2 cups finely chopped onions
½ cup finely chopped green pepper
1 tablespoon finely chopped garlic
2 cups chicken stock, fresh or canned (more stock may be added)
½ pound lean cooked smoked ham, sliced ½-inch thick and cut into
    ½-inch cubes
2 16-ounce cans tomatoes, drained and coarsely chopped with all liquid
    reserved
3 medium-sized yams (1 pound), peeled and cut into 1-inch chunks
4 fresh parsley sprigs and 1 large bay leaf tied together
¼ teaspoon ground cayenne pepper
1 pound fresh okra, washed, trimmed and cut crosswide into 1-inch
    thick rounds

*Pat the cubes of veal dry with paper towels and season with 1 teaspoon salt
and ¼ teaspoon black pepper. Roll 1 piece at a time in flour to coat lightly.
Shake off excess flour.*

*In a heavy 12-inch skillet, melt butter with ¼ cup oil over medium heat.
When foam begins to subside, add about half the veal and brown, turning
the pieces frequently to color richly and evenly without burning. When first
batch of veal is browned, transfer to a heavy 8-quart casserole and brown
remaining veal adding up to ¼ cup more oil if necessary.*

*Pour off all but a thin film of fat from skillet and add onions, green pepper
and garlic. Stirring frequently, cook over medium heat for about 5 minutes
or until vegetables are soft but not brown. Transfer vegetables to the
casserole with the veal. Pour chicken stock into skillet and bring to a boil
over high heat, meanwhile scraping in any brown particles from pan. Pour
stock mixture over veal.*

*Stir ham, tomatoes, yams, parsley and bay leaf, red pepper and the remaining teaspoon of salt into veal mixture and bring to a boil. Reduce heat to low,
cover the casserole partially and simmer for 1½ hours. Stir in the okra and
simmer partially covered for about 30 minutes longer until the veal is tender
and shows no resistance when pierced with the point of a small sharp
knife.*

*Pick out and discard parsley and bay leaf and taste stew for seasoning.
Serve at once with rice or noodles.*
Serves: 8-10

Favorite recipe of: Tony Bently, New Orleans, Louisiana
Career Highlights: Track announcer at the Fair Grounds in New Orleans since 1974;
                        also worked at Arlington Park, Delaware Park, Monmouth Park,
                        Charlestown, Turf Paradise, Gulfstream Park and Louisiana Downs,
                        as well as at many of the nation's steeplechase race meetings.

VEAL WITH WHITE WINE AND MUSHROOMS

5 pounds boneless veal, cut into 2-3-inch pieces
½ cup butter, separated
2 tablespoons corn oil
1 large onion, chopped fine
4 tablespoons flour
2 cups dry, white wine
2 cups warm water
Salt and pepper to taste
1 teaspoon thyme or 4 bay leaves
2 pounds fresh mushrooms, sliced

In a large, deep skillet, brown veal in 6 tablespoons butter and oil. Add onion and gradually add flour stirring so that it does not lump. When flour is well blended and smooth, add wine and water and continue stirring. Add seasonings and stir until mixture boils. Reduce heat to simmer, cover and cook slowly for 1½ hours. Saute mushrooms in remaining butter. Add to veal 15 minutes before it is done. Serve over rice.

RICE

2½ cups rice
2 tablespoons butter
5 cups water

Brown rice in butter. Add water and heat to boiling. Reduce heat. Cover and simmer about 30 minutes or until rice is tender and moisture is absorbed.
Serves: 8

Origin: Martine Alford, Lyon, France
Favorite recipe of: The Editor

VEAL PARMIGIANA

4 slices lean veal
1 egg, beaten
1 tablespoon water
1 teaspoon salt
Pepper to taste
1 cup dry bread crumbs
3 tablespoon grated Parmesan cheese
6 tablespoons shortening
1 7½-ounce can tomato sauce
4 slices mozzarella cheese

Combine egg, water, salt and pepper. Blend together bread crumbs and Parmesan cheese in flat pan. Dip each slice of veal in egg mixture, then in bread crumbs. Heat shortening in a heavy frying pan. Brown meat in pan over moderate heat. When meat is browned on both sides, Pour off excess fat. Pour tomato sauce around meat not over it. Top each piece of meat with 1 slice mozzarella cheese. Cover pan and cook slowly for 35-40 minutes adding water if necessary. Spoon sauce over meat when serving.
Serves: 4

Origin: Tony "Bonesy" Cappola
Favorite recipe of: Abigail Fuller, New England Native
Career Highlights: Regular rider of *Mom's Command,* winner of the New York
Filly Triple Crown (Acorn, Mother Goose and Coaching Club
American Oaks), 1985.

TEE RED'S BARBECUED CHICKEN

2 large fryers, cut in serving pieces
1 cup ketchup
1 clove garlic, finely minced
¼ cup butter or olive oil
½ cup beer
2 tablespoons sugar
Red pepper, to taste
Salt, to taste

Boil chicken pieces until almost done. Place chicken in broiler pan. Mix ketchup, garlic, butter or oil, beer, sugar, pepper and salt in a saucepan and simmer until flavors blend. Baste chicken pieces with sauce. Broil 15 minutes on each side, basting often. Serve with hot garlic French bread.
Serves: 6

Favorite recipe of: Glyn P. (Tee Red) Bernis, Louisiana native
Career Highlights: Champion Jockey in 1964. Leading Trainer at
Louisiana Downs 2 years.

ITALIAN CHICKEN

8 skinned chicken breasts
Olive oil
Salt and pepper to taste
2 tablespoons minced garlic
⅓ cup fresh parsley, chopped
Juice of 1 or 2 lemons
1 teaspoon Italian seasoning
½ cup butter or margarine

Brush chickens lightly with olive oil and season with salt and pepper. Mix together in a saucepan over low heat: garlic, parsley, lemon juice, Italian seasoning, butter and 2 tablespoons olive oil. Place chicken bone side up in broiler pan. Set oven on Broil at 400°. Brush chicken with sauce. Broil for approximately 10 minutes, then baste with sauce and turn over. Broil meat side up for approximately 15 minutes basting with sauce so meat does not dry out. Serve with Sauteed Mushrooms.

SAUTEED MUSHROOMS

½ cup butter or margarine
2 tablespoons olive oil
1 pound fresh mushrooms, sliced
2 tablespoons fresh parsley, chopped
1 bunch green onions, chopped
1 large onion, chopped
1 tablespoon fresh garlic, chopped
Juice of 1½ lemons
Salt and pepper to taste

Saute mushrooms in ½ of butter and olive oil for 5 minutes. Add seasonings, parsley, onions, garlic and remaining butter. Continue to saute stirring occasionally until onions are clear. Serve with Italian Chicken.

Original recipe of: Vincent Timphony, Owner-Trainer, New Orleans native
Career Highlights: Trainer and part owner of *Wild Again,* winner of the Inaugural
Breeder's Cup Classic at Hollywood Park. Former owner of
Vincenzo's Restaurant in New Orleans.

CHICKEN CACCIATORE

1 chicken, cut up and dusted with flour
Oil or butter for browning
1 bell pepper, cut in strips
1 can stewed tomatoes, or 3-4 fresh tomatoes
1 onion, sliced
Salt and pepper to taste
¼ teaspoon garlic powder
1 bay leaf
1 teaspoon Italian seasoning

On top of stove, brown chicken in oil or butter. Add rest of ingredients and cook over low heat 2-3 hours until done.
Serves: 3-4

Origin: Marilyn Karuza, private secretary to E. W. Johnston, developed this recipe
for Mr. Johnston and his family.
Favorite recipe of: E. W. Johnston, Owner, Old English Rancho, Ontario, California.

MEXICAN CHICKEN CHALLENGE

"Quick and delicious microwave chicken dish"

4 whole chicken breasts, deboned and skin removed
3 tablespoons Old English Cheese spread
3 tablespoons butter
2 tablespoons chopped green chilies
2 teaspoons grated onion
1 teaspoon salt
1 teaspoon MSG
1 cup crushed Cheese Nips
1½ tablespoons taco seasoning (more for hot taste)
¼-½ cup melted butter

Divide each whole breast into 2. Pound each piece with a mallet until thin and set aside. Beat butter and cheese spread until well blended. Mix in onion, salt, MSG and chilies. Divide mixture into 8 equal parts. Place portion of cheese mixture on end of each chicken breast and roll up; tuck in ends and secure with toothpicks. Mix crushed Cheese Nips with taco seasoning. Dip chicken roll in melted butter and roll in crushed cheese crumbs. Place in pyrex baking dish and cover with waxed paper. Microwave on high for 10-12 minutes. Serve with chopped, fresh tomatoes, shredded lettuce, J. J.'s Guacamole Dip and corn chips.
Serves: 4-6

Favorite recipe of: J. J. Pletcher, Trainer, Benton, Louisiana
Career Highlights: Trainer of over 30 stakes winners including such horses as *Uncool, Circle of Steel, Lockjaw, Double Line, Breaker Breaker* and *Limited Edition.*

"Challenge — To vie for the lead."

CHICKEN ENCHILADA CASSEROLE

2 chickens, cooked, boned and diced (or equivalent of all white meat)
2 cans cream of mushroom soup
2 cans cream of celery soup
2 cans cream of chicken soup
1 8-ounce package cream cheese
1 8-ounce carton sour cream
1 onion, minced
2 4-ounce cans green chilies, seeded and chopped
2 packages corn tortillas
Cheddar cheese, grated

Cook chicken and save broth. Debone and dice. Combine cream cheese, sour cream and minced onion. Mix well with soups. Add chicken and chilies. Heat broth and dip tortillas until limp. Layer casserole with tortillas and chicken mixture; layer until all is used. Cover generously with grated cheese. Bake at 350° for 45 minutes. Freezes well.
Serves: 20

Origin: Mrs. Cloyce K. (Fern) Box, Frisco, Texas and
     Mr. Rick Brasher, Haughton, Louisiana
Options: Rick eliminates the cream of celery soup, cream cheese and sour cream from
     his recipe and adds chopped water chestnuts and crushed garlic.
     Both are delicious!
Favorite recipe of: Thoroughbred Owner, Cloyce K. Box and
     Thoroughbred Trainer, Rick Brasher

ODDS ON FAVORITE CHICKEN ENCHILADAS

8 flour tortillas
3-4 chicken breasts
16-ounce package ricotta cheese
1 10-ounce can kernal corn
1 medium can tomato sauce
1 medium can enchilada sauce
1 cup shredded Cheddar cheese
1 cup shredded Jack cheese

Boil chicken breasts in salted water for approximately 45 minutes. Cool, throw away skin and pull small pieces of chicken from bones. Place chicken in large bowl; add ricotta and corn and mix. Spoon mixture in equal portions into flour tortillas and roll into enchiladas. Place in a large pyrex casserole pan (8x13). Mix tomato and enchilada sauces and pour over top. Spread cheeses over top and place in 350° oven for 30 to 40 minutes. Great make ahead dish. Add sauce and cheese just before baking.
Serves: 8

Favorite recipe of: Frankie Olivares, Jockey, Monrovia, California
Career Highlights: 1982 Florida Derby; rode *Little Reb* to victory over *Affirmed* in
     1978; 1977 George Woolf Award recipient.

"Odds on — Odds of less than even money."

KING RANCH CHICKEN

2 large fryers
1 chopped onion
2 stalks celery, chopped
1 bell pepper, chopped
1 package frozen tortillas
Chili powder, to taste
Garlic salt, to taste
Salt and pepper, to taste
1 can cream of chicken soup
1 can cream of mushroom soup
2 cups grated cheese
1 can Rotel tomatoes

Boil chicken until tender. Debone chicken and save stock. Boil onion, celery and bell pepper in stock until clear. Remove vegetables. Soak tortillas in stock until slightly wilted. In large casserole, line bottom with tortillas. Add half chicken tossed with vegetables. Sprinkle with chili powder, garlic salt, salt and pepper. Combine soups and spread half over chicken mixture, then half of grated cheese. Repeat layers and pour Rotel tomatoes on top. Bake uncovered at 375° for 30 minutes.
Serves: 8

Favorite recipe of: Forrest Martin, Longview, Texas
Racing interest: Thoroughbred owner and racing enthusiast.

CURRIED CHICKEN

1 3½-pound chicken cut into serving pieces
Salt and freshly ground pepper to taste
2 tablespoons oil
2 cloves garlic, finely minced
1 medium onion, chopped
1 tablespoon curry powder
1 cup chicken stock
3 fresh peaches, peeled and sliced
½ cup yogurt
Optional: Nuts (pecans or cashews), coconuts, raisins

Season chicken and brown in skillet with oil. Remove chicken and add garlic and onion to skillet and saute 3 minutes. Add curry, chicken and stock and bring to boil. Reduce heat and simmer 25 minutes. Remove chicken again. Reduce liquid by boiling 3 minutes. Add peaches and cook 1 minute, then stir in yogurt. Pour over chicken and serve. Nuts, coconut or raisins may be added as condiments.
Serves: 4

Origin: Mary Gates, Hot Springs, Arkansas
Favorite recipe of: Sam Maple, Jockey, Hot Springs, Arkansas
Career Highlights: Being regular rider of *Smart Angle*, 2-year-old Eclipse Award winning filly in 1979. She was trained by Woody Stephens and owned by Mr. and Mrs. Jim Ryan.

LE POULET A LA CREME

1 whole chicken, cut into four pieces
¼ cup butter
1 onion, chopped
1 cup thick cream
2 egg yolks
Juice of 1 lemon

Melt butter in a heavy pan. Add chopped onion and the pieces of chicken and cook slowly. When it is nearly done, cover chicken with cream and let it bubble for 10 minutes. Remove chicken and keep hot in a serving dish. Beat the yolks and lemon juice into the sauce in the pan and let it thicken. Pour sauce through a fine sieve onto the chicken.
Serves: 4

Origin: Madame Brajier of Brajier's Restaurant, one of the famous restaurants of
      Lyon, France.
Favorite recipe of: Alec Head, Trainer and Breeder, Chantilly, France
Career Highlights: Alec Head's ancestors have been professional trainers and jockeys
      for nearly 150 years. A trainer since 1947, Head has won more
      than 20 French classics, as well as five in Ireland. In Britain
      he has won the Derby, the 2,000 Guineas and 1,000 Guineas, as
      well as the King George VI and Queen Elizabeth Stakes. Besides
      these and the Prix de l'Arc de Triomphe, he has won nearly
      every major race in Europe. Head also has a great interest in
      breeding running a 500-acre stud farm in Normandy, France.

HEAVENLY CHICKEN

2 small whole fryers (2-2¼ pounds each)
Salt and pepper to taste
1 apple, cut in half, then quartered
2 large Spanish onions, quartered
2 sticks butter
Sweet and sour sparerib sauce

Clean chickens well, inside and out. Salt and pepper to taste, inside and out. Insert half of apple and half of 1 onion, both quartered, inside each chicken. Rub chickens thoroughly on outside with butter. Dot remaining butter on outside of chickens. Put remaining quartered onion on top of chickens. Place in 220° oven, uncovered. Baste as frequently as possible throughout cooking time. Cook for 4 hours. The last half hour, cover entire chickens with sweet and sour sauce.
Serves: 4-6

Original recipe of: Renee Yowell, Raintree Farm, Ocala, Florida
Career Highlights: Breeder of Stakes Thoroughbreds: *Delphic Oracle, Proud Appeal,*
      Swede Shoes, Bold Rendezvous, Timely Council,
      WhatsYourPleasure, Star Hitch, Iron Streak, Iron Derby,
      Khal On Me, Unknown Lady, In A Trance, Fast Music, Miss
      Hurricane and *Kilbegan.*

MUCH THE BEST CHICKEN BROCCOLI CASSEROLE

2 cans cream of mushroom soup
2 6-ounce jars cheese spread
4-6 boneless chicken breasts, cooked and cut into chunks
3 10-ounce packages chopped broccoli, thawed
2 cups cooked rice
1 cup chopped celery
1 cup chopped onion
1 teaspoon salt

Combine soup and cheese in a saucepan over low heat. Gently fold in remaining ingredients. Pour into greased baking dish. Bake in a preheated 325° oven for 45 minutes — 1 hour.
Serves: 8-10

Favorite recipe of: Kathleen M. Moore, Jockey
Career Highlights: Rider of *Gallant Serenade,* winner of the King Cotton Handicap in 1981; won the Hot Springs Handicap aboard *Skate* in 1982; won the Dixie Miss Stakes in 1983 aboard *Big Dreams;* aboard *Picture Point* in the Reflection Stakes in 1984; Rode in Japan for 30 days in the International Ladies Cup Challenge in 1982.

CHICKEN AND BROCCOLI CASSEROLE

8 chicken breasts, cooked and cut into bite size pieces
2 packages frozen broccoli spears, or 1 large bunch fresh broccoli
2 cans cream of chicken soup, or 2 cans cream of celery soup
1 cup mayonnaise
1 teaspoon curry powder
1 teaspoon lemon juice
1 cup herb seasoned stuffing mix, or 1 cup soft whole wheat bread
    cubes tossed in 2 tablespoons melted butter
Optional: Shredded cheese for topping

Cook broccoli according to package directions or if using fresh, steam until just tender but firm. Rub casserole with margarine. Place broccoli pieces to cover bottom of dish. Place chicken pieces on top of broccoli. Mix together soup, mayonnaise, curry powder and lemon juice to make sauce. Pour over chicken and broccoli. Sprinkle with dressing or bread cubes and cheese, if desired. Bake at 350° for approximately 25-30 minutes.
Serves: 6-8
Editor's Note: **We may have uncovered the secret recipe for success! This Chicken and Broccoli Casserole recipe was sent to me as the favorite recipe of leading Thoroughbred owner, John Franks and leading trainer, Woody Stephens. Another possibility is that Alta Franks and Lucille Stephens are "recipe-trading" friends.**

CHURCHILL CHICKEN BREASTS

12 skinned and deboned chicken breasts
12 slices bacon
1 large jar dried beef
12 ounces sour cream
1 10-ounce can cream of chicken soup
Dash red pepper
1 bunch green onions, chopped

Wrap each breast in bacon and place in 9x12-inch baking dish which has been lined with dried beef. Mix sour cream, soup, pepper and green onions and pour over chicken breasts. Cover and bake at 275° for 2 hours. Remove cover and cook 15 or 20 minutes longer at 350°.
Serves: 12

Origin: Mrs. Larry (Becky U.) Melancon
Favorite recipe of: Larry J. Melancon, Jockey, Louisville, Kentucky
Career Highlights: Rider of *Come Summer,* winner of the first running of the Canterbury
Derby, Canterbury Down, Shakopee, Minnesota

GUISO DE POLLO CON ZANAHORIA
(Stewed Chicken With Carrots)

8 pieces chicken
3 tablespoons corn oil, more if needed
1 onion, chopped
1 tomato, chopped
1 teaspoon minced garlic
½ cup sliced carrots
1 teaspoon ground red pepper
½ teaspoon oregano
Salt, to taste

Fry chicken until brown in corn oil. Remove chicken and set aside. In remaining oil, saute onion, tomato, garlic, carrots, red pepper, oregano, and salt. Saute mixture about 5 minutes. Set chicken pieces on top and add ½ cup water. Cover and cook for about 30 minutes on low heat. Serve over rice.
Serves: 4

Origin: Lima, Peru
Favorite recipe of: Fernando Valdizan, Trainer, Bossier City, Louisiana

PAELLA A LA VALENCIANA
(Chicken and Seafood Rice)

6 cups very strong chicken broth, preferably homemade
½ teasppon saffron
1 small onion, peeled
2 small chickens, about 2½ pounds each
Coarse salt
½ cup olive oil
¼ pound chorizo sausage, in ¼-inch slices
1 large pork chop, boned and diced
1 medium onion, chopped
4 scallions, chopped
4 cloves garlic, minced
2 pimentos, diced
1 pound small or medium shrimp, shelled
4 lobster tails, split lengthwise or 8 king crab claws
3 cups short-grain rice
5 tablespoons chopped parsley
2 bay leaves, crumbled
½ cup dry white wine
1 tablespoon lemon juice
¼ pound fresh or frozen peas
18 clams, smallest available, at room temperature, scrubbed
18 small mussels, scrubbed
Lemon wedges for garnish
Parsley for garnish

Heat broth with saffron and whole onion. Cover and simmer 15 minutes. Remove onion and measure broth; you need exactly 5½ cups. Cut chicken into small serving pieces (the whole breast into 4 parts, each thigh into 2 parts, the bony tip of the leg chopped off, the wing tip discarded, and the rest of the wing separated into 2 parts.) Dry the pieces well and sprinkle with salt. In a metal paella pan, with about a 15-inch base, heat oil. Add the chicken pieces and fry over high heat until golden. Remove to a warm platter. Add the chorizo, pork and ham to the pan and stir fry about 10 minutes. Add the chopped onion, scallions, garlic, and pimentos and saute until the onion is wilted. Add the shrimp and lobster and saute about 3 minutes more, or until shrimp and lobster barely turn pink. Remove the shrimp and lobster to the platter with the chicken. Add the rice to the pan and stir to coat it well with oil. Sprinkle in chopped parsley and bay leaves. (Make in advance up to this point.)

Stir in the chicken broth, boiling hot, the wine, lemon juice and peas. Salt to taste. Bring to a boil and cook, uncovered and stirring occasionally, over medium-high heat about 10 minutes. Bury the shrimp and chicken in the rice. Add the clams and mussels, pushing them into the rice, with the edge that will open facing up. Decorate the paella with the lobster pieces, then bake at 325°, uncovered, for 20 minutes. Remove from the oven and let sit on top of stove, lightly covered with foil, for about 10 minutes. Decorate each serving with lemon wedges and parsley.
Serves: 8-10

Favorite recipe of: Joe Ferrer, Jockey Agent, New Orleans, Louisiana

THERE'S ONLY ONE WAY TO ROAST A TURKEY/DUCK/GOOSE...
(even if there is 101 ways to lose a horse race...)

1 fresh bird
6-8 stalks celery, chopped
3 large carrots, chopped fine
Chicken stock
Salt and pepper, to taste
Sage
Celery seed
French bread
½ cup butter
1 large onion, chopped
1 clove garlic, pressed
Soda crackers
Optional: Oysters for dressing

If at all possible, get a FRESH bird; freezing destroys much of the taste. If that isn't possible, defrost in the refrigerator, testing each day (according to poundage) its readiness.

Remove the giblets from the turkey, or whatever. Discard liver unless someone in the crowd is very fond of it. Then leave it aside to cook in a little gravy later. Take heart, gizzard and neck, place in large kettle and add 4-5 stalks chopped celery, 2 large chopped (very fine) carrots and cover with ½ water and ½ chicken stock. Bring to a boil. Add salt and pepper to taste, plus a dash of sage and celery seed. Simmer until the stock reduces by at least one-half.

In meantime, make DRESSING. The evening ahead, make croutons: Cut large pieces of French bread into bite-size pieces; allow to become somewhat stale. When ready (crisp to bite) melt butter, and the following which has been prepared ahead of time: Chicken broth in which 2-3 celery stalks, 1 large carrot and 1 large onion have been chopped. Add salt and pepper to taste, plus 2½ teaspoons sage. At the last minute before stuffing, take garlic press and add garlic to the mixture. Add vegetables and enough liquid and butter to soften mixture.* Stuff and truss the bird.

Cook bird at 325° according to poundage; a meat thermometer still being the most reliable source for doneness. If bird becomes too brown, cover top with foil, but continue to baste with juices.

When broth of giblets has been reduced, skim any residue from top and discard the giblets. Take broth, including vegetables and 1 cup at a time place in blender or food processor with the following proportions: 1 cup broth to 4 soda crackers. If mixture looks too thin or too thick, use your discretion, adding a cracker or 2 at a time until desired consistency is reached.

This gravy MAY be prepared the day ahead and refrigerated if desired. When the turkey/duck/goose is done, pour off most of fat and add gravy mixture (brought to room temperature) to drippings until brown; it may be seasoned with salt and pepper to taste.

*For those fans who despise oysters, but like oyster stuffing, here is a suggestion: A tablespoon or 2 of the juice, or 'liqueor' if you prefer, can be used in conjunction with 1 or 2 oysters chopped briefly in the blender. The taste is there, but the oysters aren't.

Every family has his own traditions, so serve your bird with cranberry sauce, home-made noodles and desserts of date pudding or pumpkin pie. The secret is to be thankful for what you've got that special November day— even if it's just one winner.

Favorite recipe of: Ellen Parker, Freelance Thoroughbred Writer, Oakland, California

STARTER/ALLOWANCE DRESSING

2 10 or 12-ounce packages cornbread mix
2 pounds sausage (at least 1 pound hot)
4 cups chopped celery
3 cups chopped onion
1 cup chopped green pepper
¾ cup chopped parsley
1½ teaspoons rubbed savory
1½ teaspoon sage leaves
1½ teaspoon dried thyme
1 tablespoon salt
½ teaspoon pepper
1 13¾-ounce can chicken broth, undiluted
3 eggs, slightly beaten

Prepare cornbread according to package directions and cool. Saute sausage. When done, remove sausage from pan and set aside. In drippings, saute celery, onion, green pepper and parsley for about 6 minutes. Crumble cornbread and add sausage, vegetables and spices. Gradually add broth and eggs, tossing lightly with fork. Use as poultry stuffing or bake in greased baking dish at 325° until thoroughly heated.
Yield: About 15 cups

Favorite recipe of: Howard L. Battle, Racing Secretary, Keeneland Race Course,
                    Lexington, Kentucky

"Allowance race — A non-claiming affair in which published conditions stipulate weight allowances according to previous purse earnings and/or number or type of victories."

GRAM'S OYSTER STUFFING

Turkey liver and heart, minced
½ cup butter or margarine
2 large onions, minced
½ bunch green onions, minced
1 bay leaf
1 sprig thyme
½ cup celery, minced
3 cloves garlic, minced
4 teaspoons minced parsley
3 dozen small oysters, cut in half
1 loaf French bread
2 teaspoons salt
¼ teaspoon black pepper
2 eggs, slightly beaten

Brown liver and heart in butter or margarine in skillet over low heat, about 15 minutes. Add onions, bay leaf, thyme and celery. Cook until tender over low heat, about 20 minutes. Add garlic, parsley and oysters. Cook until almost all water leaves oysters, about 15 minutes. Remove bay leaf and thyme. Place bread under cold running water; press out excess moisture with hands. Break bread into small pieces and add to oyster mixture. Stir and cook until thoroughly heated, about 15 minutes. Remove from heat, add salt, pepper and eggs. Mix well. Stuff in turkey or bake in covered casserole at 350° for 30 minutes.
Yield: Stuffing for 10-pound turkey

Origin: Mrs. Myrtle Tangue, New Orleans, Louisiana
Favorite recipe of: The Editor

POSITIVE CHICKEN or QUARTER POLE LIVER

2 tomatoes, chopped
1 green bell pepper, sliced or chopped
1 sweet onion, sliced or chopped
3 stalks celery, sliced or chopped
¾-1 cup water
½ teaspoon pepper
¼ teaspoon salt
Garlic salt, to taste
2 medium chicken breasts or 1 pound sliced liver

Add vegetables to water in a medium saucepan. Bring to a low simmer and add spices. Add chicken or liver cut up into thin slices ¼ inch thick, 2 inches long or 1-inch squares. bring to boil, then simmer for approximately 15-20 minutes or until water starts to thicken. Stir occasionally. Serve with boiled potatoes or over whole grain brown rice. Don's favorite is over rice.

BROWN RICE: About ½ cup whole grain brown rice
*   1½ cups water*
Boil water and rice for 1 minute and then simmer, covered, for 30 minutes,
Makes 3 ½-cup servings.
Serves: 2-3

Original recipe of: Donald Macbeth, Jockey, Garden City, New York
                    "Cooking on the road is a bachelor's survival."
Career Highlights: Leading rider at Monmouth Park for three years; leading rider
                    at Atlantic City, Meadowlands, Hialeah, Aqueduct for two years.
                    Won Flamingo aboard *Bushongo;* won Suburban on
                    Temperence Hill; rode *Silver Buck* for track record in 1982;
                    rode *Deputy Minister* in two-year-old Eclipse year.
                    Won the 1985 Marlboro Cup aboard *Chief's Crown.*

"Quarter Pole — Colored pole at infield rail exactly two furlongs from finish wire."

LIVER IN BASIL BUTTER

1-1½ pounds calves liver, cut in ¼-inch slices
Flour for dredging
1 bunch fresh basil
½ cup softened butter
2 teaspoon fresh chopped parsley
1 large colve garlic, chopped
½ cup dry white wine
Salt and pepper to taste

In a blender jar, combine the basil, butter, parsley, wine, salt and pepper. Blend until smooth. Dredge the liver in flour. Place an iron skillet over moderate heat. When hot, drop in 1 tablespoon basil butter. After the butter has melted, drop in 2 or 3 slices of liver, depending on size of skillet. Saute for 1 minute, then turn. Place a sizable dollop of the basil butter on the top side of the liver. After 1 minute, turn again and smother with basil butter. Saute for a total of 3-4 minutes taking care not to overcook. Repeat with the remainder of the slices.
Serves: 4

Favorite recipe of: Bennett Parke, Director of Racing, Detroit Race Course,
            Livonia, Michigan

SWEETBREADS AVGOLEMONO SAUCE

1 pint chicken broth
3 egg yolks
1 whole egg
¼ cup lemon juice, freshly squeezed
2 pounds sweetbreads
2 tablespoons butter
4 tablespoons olive oil
¼ teaspoon salt
⅛ teaspoon garlic salt
¼ teaspoon white pepper
1 quart water
Parsley, chopped fine for garnish

For Avgolemono Sauce, heat broth over low heat. Beat eggs until light lemon color. Add lemon juice while whipping. Remove broth from heat and add egg mixture slowly, stirring constantly. Keep warm. Parboil the sweetbreads in water with condiments for 15 minutes, remove and immediately immerse in ice water, remove and skin. After skinning and deveining, cut sweetbreads into 1¼-inch pieces. Saute at medium heat in butter and olive oil in black iron skillet for about 15 minutes, turning constantly. Establish portions of 3 or 4 sweetbreads per serving. Pour warm sauce over and serve with small forks. Garnish with parsley.
Serves: 6

Origin: Ancient Sephardic recipe from the island of Rhodes
Favorite recipe of: Morris J. Alhadeff, President, Washington Jockey Club,
            Operators of Longacres Race Track, Renton, Washington

DOC'S FAVORITE SHRIMP

1 onion, chopped
2 pods garlic, chopped fine
1 teaspoon fresh basil, chopped
2 tablespoons fresh parsley, chopped
¼ cup olive oil
3 chopped tomatoes, peeled and seeded
2 pounds raw shrimp, peeled
Red pepper, to taste

Combine all fresh ingredients (except shrimp) in a large saucepan with oil. Heat and stir until onions are almost clear. Season to taste, then add shrimp. Cook only until shrimp are pink, about 3-4 minutes. Don't overcook! Good served with pasta or with rice on the side.
Serves: 4-6

Favorite recipe of: Doc Severinsen, "Tonight Show", Burbank, California
Racing interest: Thoroughbred Owner and racing enthusiast. Doc jokes, "You've heard of the Galloping Gourmet; well, I'm the Trotting Trumpeter."
Enjoys cooking with his wife, Emily.

SHRIMP LA'RUE

3 pounds extra large shrimp, peeled
1 bottle dill sauce
4 tablespoons butter
¼ cup white wine
½ cup barbecue sauce
2 tablespoons garlic salt
½ tablespoon cayenne pepper
2 tablespoons black pepper
1 tablespoon minced parsley
2 boxes long grain and wild rice
1 pound fresh mushrooms, sliced
2 large onions, chopped
2 cups chopped green pepper
2 cloved garlic, minced

Marinate shrimp in dill sauce for 3 hours. Place shrimp on skewer and pre-heat grill. Make barbecue sauce by blending together over low heat: butter, wine, and barbecue sauce. Dust shrimp with seasoning. Place on grill and cook 3 minutes on each side, basting cooked side with barbecue sauce. Baste again with sauce before placing on bed of rice.
Rice: Cook rice according to package directions, adding sauteed onions, peppers, mushrooms and garlic.
Serves: 6

Favorite recipe of: Lawrence M. Schafer, Assistant Maitre'd at Louisiana
Downs' Pelican Room, Bossier City, Louisiana

SHRIMP RAYMOND

3 pounds large shrimp, cooked, peeled and deveined
½ cup butter
2 medium bell peppers, cut int thin strips
4 large pimentos, sliced in slivers
1 cup all-purpose flour
1 quart light cream
2 cups shredded Cheddar cheese
Tabasco, dash or to taste
1 teaspoon salt
½ teaspoon white pepper
½ cup good dry sherry

Prepare shrimp and set aside. In a saucepan, melt butter and saute bell peppers and pimento slivers for about 20 minutes, until tender. Gradually add the flour and continue to cook until roux is blended. Slowly add the cream and continue cooking until sauce thickens slightly. Add cheese a little at a time and continue to cook until sauce is well blended and thick. Add Tabasco, salt, pepper and sherry. Combine sauce with the shrimp and serve immediately with Green Rice.
Serves: 8

Origin: Original recipe of the late Raymond F. Salmen
Favorite recipe of: Jeanne S. Salmen, New Orleans, Louisiana
Career Highlights: Jeanne and Raymond Salmen owned and raced thoroughbreds
since 1969. The greatest horse that raced in the Salmen colors was
A Letter To Harry who won numerous stakes races all over
the country.

SHRIMP GRAND CHENIER

5 pounds headless, jumbo shrimp, in shells
1 pound melted butter or margarine
6 tablespoon black pepper
1 large bottle Wishbone Italian dressing
Juice of 2 lemons

Place shrimp in large roasting pan. Mix remaining ingredients together and pour over shrimp. Bake uncovered at 400° for 40 minutes, turning gently every 10 minutes. Serve with hot French bread. Serve sauce from roaster in individual bowls for dipping bread.
Serves: 6

Favorite recipe of: Forrest Martin, Thoroughbred Owner, Longview, Texas

SHRIMP AND RICE

3 pounds medium shrimp, boiled
2 cans sliced mushrooms or ½ pound fresh mushrooms, sliced
¾ cup butter
½ cup chopped parsley
4 tablespoons chopped onions
2 tablespoons lemon juice
2 tablespoons chili sauce or cocktail sauce
1 teaspoon salt
½ teaspoon garlic salt
Dash Worcestershire sauce
Dash hot sauce
1 box long grain and wild rice

Saute parsley and onions until onions are clear. Add mushrooms, lemon juice, chili sauce and all seasonings. Add shrimp and mix well. Remove from heat and set aside while preparing rice. Cook rice according to package directions. When done, combine rice and shrimp mixture and place in casserole. Bake in 350° oven for 20-30 minutes.
Serves: 6

Favorite recipe of: Erma Hicks, Benton, Louisiana
Racing interest: Horesman's Bookkeeper at Louisiana Downs and Oaklawn Park

FORREST'S FAVORITE SHRIMP CREOLE

½ cup chopped green onions
3 garlic cloves, minced
⅓ cup salad oil
¼ cup flour
1 8-ounce can tomato sauce
1 7-ounce bottle lemon-lime soda
2 pounds medium shrimp, uncooked
2 bay leaves
1 teaspoon salt
½ teaspoon thyme

Saute onions and garlic in oil about 5 minutes. Stir in flour until well blended. Add tomato sauce and soda. Cook over low heat stirring until mixture boils. Add shrimp, bay leaves, salt and thyme. Cook over low heat 15 minutes stirring occasionally. Remove bay leaves and serve over cooked rice.
Serves: 4

Origin: Mrs. Forrest (Betty) Kaelin, Finchville, Kentucky
Favorite recipe of: Forrest Kaelin, Trainer

SCAMPI TO WIN

1½ pounds uncooked jumbo shrimp
1 pound butter or margarine
10 cloves garlic
⅛ teaspoon Tabasco
¼ teaspoon salt
2 teaspoons chopped chervil
½ teaspoon paprika
½ teaspoon cracked Java black pepper

Clean and devein shrimp, leaving tails on. Melt butter or margarine. Put garlic through press and use juice as well as pulp. Add all other ingredients to butter and garlic to heat. Place shrimp in glass baking dish in rows (can be layered). Pour sauce over shrimp so it is completely covered. Leave shrimp in sauce at least 3-4 hours for flavor to be absorbed. (At this point it can all be frozen to use later; be sure to cover well if put in freezer.) Refrigerate, covered. When ready to cook take dish out of refrigerator so butter will soften somewhat. Carefully put shrimp and sauce in skillet to cook. Do a few at a time so as not to crowd them while cooking. Cook on both sides about 3-5 minutes. Can be served with noodles or rice or used as an appetizer.
Serves: 3-4

Original recipe of: Dr. Ed Giammarino, Glendale, California
Racing interest: An Optometrist by profession, Ed Giammarino is an avid race fan and excellent cook. He and his wife enjoy entertaining their friends in racing with parties and dinners. This is one recipe that is always a big hit.

SHRIMP MOSCA

8 ounces olive oil
Black pepper
8-10 cloves garlic, cut in half
3 tablespoons rosemary
5 bay leaves
Cayenne pepper, to taste
2 tablespoons salt
3 pounds raw, headless shrimp, unpeeled
¾ cup sauterne
French bread

Pour oil into large pot with lid. Cover the top of oil with black pepper. Add next 5 ingredients and simmer over low heat until garlic is brown, 10-15 minutes. Add shrimp and increase heat. Stir almost constantly until shrimp are pink, 8-10 minutes. Lower heat, add sauterne and stir. Cover and simmer another 10 minutes, stirring occasionally. Serve in bowls with bread on the side. Peel, then dip the peeled shrimp in bowl of sauce. Bread dipped in sauce is delicious!
Serves: 6

Favorite recipe of: Jerry Hissam, Hot Springs, Arkansas
Career Highlights: Racing Official for six years; Jockey Agent for 14 years.

GARDEN STATE SEAFOOD CASSEROLE

1 cup seafood (use your favorite)
1 can cream of shrimp soup
1 cup mayonnaise
2 cups cooked noodles
½ cup lightly sauteed mushrooms
3 tablespoons sherry
¼ cup shredded sharp Cheddar cheese

Combine first 6 ingredients in casserole. Top with cheese. Bake in 350° oven for 45 minutes or until hot. Can be prepared ahead and baked when needed.
Serves: 4

Favorite recipe of: Jessie Pohlhaus, Owner, Sherwood Manor Farm,
Claiborne, Maryland

MONA'S SHRIMP AND MUSHROOM CASSEROLE

¾ cup butter
½ bunch green onions, tops and bottoms, chopped
½ small bell pepper, chopped
1 small onion, chopped
2 pounds peeled shrimp
Salt, red and black pepper, to taste
Garlic powder, to taste
1 can sliced mushrooms, or ½ pound fresh sliced mushrooms
Flour
Light cream
½ cup shredded Cheddar cheese
Parmesan cheese
Bread crumbs

In a large pan, melt butter and add chopped vegetables. Saute 2-3 minutes, then add raw shrimp which have been seasoned with salt, peppers and garlic powder. Add mushrooms and saute along with shrimp. Cook until shrimp are pink and done. Sprinkle with flour, about 3-4 tablespoons; you want a thick, cheesy texture. Stir and add cream until smooth. Add Cheddar cheese and stir until blended. Place in small, individual casseroles and top with Parmesan and bread crumbs.
Serves: 4

Origin: Mrs. Gerald (Mona) Romero, Haughton, Louisiana
Favorite recipe of: Gerald Romero, Trainer
Career Highlights: Enjoyed his best Louisiana Downs meeting in 1984 with 40
victories to rank third in the standings; set local record for win
percentage (30.3%) in 1984.

SHRIMP DRESSING

1 pound lean ground beef
1 onion, chopped
1 bell pepper, chopped
¼ cup chopped green onion
1 pound peeled raw shrimp or crawfish
1 can cream of mushroom soup
1 package onion soup mix
1 cup raw rice

Brown meat with onion, bell pepper and green onion. Drain fat and add shrimp or crawfish, soups and rice. Stir well and cover. Bake at 350° for 1 hour, stirring after ½ hour.
Serves: 6

Favorite recipe of: Randy Romero, Jockey, Lafayette, Louisiana Native
Career Highlights: One of only two jockeys to ride in both the Kentucky Derby
and the All-American Futurity (Terry Lipham is the other); set a state
record for wins at one meeting with 181 victories at the 1983-84
Fair Grounds meeting; won his second straight Fair Grounds Title
in 1984-85; two-time riding champion at Louisiana Downs
(1979 and 1980); won riding titles at Keeneland (twice),
Churchill Downs and Arlington Park (1982); captured the
1984 Ruffian Handicap at Belmont Park and the Ladies
Handicap at Aqueduct aboard *Heatherten.*

SEA GIRT IMPERIAL

1 pound back fin crab meat
4-5 tablespoons mayonnaise
Pepper, to taste
1 cup shredded sharp cheese
Optional: Salt, to taste, chopped peppers

Sift through crab meat to remove any cartilage or shell. Add mayonnaise and pepper to taste. You may also add chopped peppers and salt if you wish. Mix well and place in a shallow baking dish or 4 individual baking dishes, no more than 1 inch deep. Sprinkle cheese over top. Place under broiler 8-10 minutes, no more. Delicious!
Serves: 4

Origin: John V. Hennegan's parents, who owned the famous
Thompson's Sea Girt House where he was born.
Favorite recipe of: John V. Hennegan, American Trainers Association, Inc.
Towson, Maryland

A CRAB CASSEROLE THAT WILL CHANGE YOUR MIND ABOUT SEAFOOD

6 stalks celery, chopped
2 medium onions, chopped
1 large green bell pepper, chopped
1½ cups vegetable oil
¾ cup flour
Dash ground white pepper
Dash nutmeg
3 tablespoons dry mustard
1½ quarts scalded milk
2 pounds crab meat, or a mixture of white fish and crab meat
Fresh grated Parmesan cheese
Paprika, preferably Hungarian sweet
Melted butter

Cook vegetables in oil until tender. Add flour, stirring constantly. Add pepper, nutmeg and mustard. Continue stirring and add hot scalded milk. Stir until thick and smooth. Add crab/mixture and stir until boiling. Remove from heat. Place in oven-proof pan. Top with grated cheese and paprika. Pour melted butter over all. Bake at 400° until bubbly, about 10 minutes. This is an extremely RICH dish which is best complimented with a light green salad or a simply prepared green vegetable.
Serves: 8

Favorite recipe of: Ellen Parker, Freelance Thoroughbred Writer,
Oakland, California

MARYDEL'S CRABMEAT CASSEROLE

2 cups chopped onions
2 cups herb seasoned stuffing mix
2 cups mayonnaise
2 cups heavy cream
1-1½ pounds back fin crab meat

Mix all ingredients together and place in a casserole dish. Bake uncovered in a 350-375° oven for 45 minutes or until heated through and brown around the edges.
Serves: 6-8

Favorite recipe of: Mary R. Odom, Marydel Farm, Middleton, Delaware

CRAB CAKES PIMLICO

1 pound backfin Maryland crab meat, well picked over
1 teaspoon grated onion
1 slice white bread, soaked in cream   *Don't use fake crab*
1 egg
1 teaspoon salt
1 teaspoon white pepper
Dash cayenne pepper
1 teaspoon dry mustard
Dash Worcestershire sauce
Flour to coat cakes
Garnish: Chopped parsley, Lemon wedges

Beat into softened bread (crust removed), egg, salt, white pepper, cayenne, dry mustard, Worcestershire and grated onion. Mix this paste well with crab meat. Make cakes about 2½ inches in diameter and ¾ inch thick. Dust lightly with flour and fry in butter until browned on both sides. Sprinkle with chopped parsley and garnish with lemon wedges. Can be served on toast or English water crackers.
Serves: 3-4

Origin: Old Maryland recipe given to Murray Friedlander by his mother
          who is now 94 years old.
Favorite recipe of: Murray Friedlander, Paris, France and Monrovia, California
Career Highlights: Longtime trainer in the United States; authority on racing abroad;
          presently spending over half the year in France, England,
          Ireland and Italy.

WINNER'S CIRCLE CRAB CAKES

1 pound crab meat
1 teaspoon seafood seasoning
8 saltine crackers, crumbled
1 teaspoon chopped parsley
2 tablespoons mayonnaise
1 teaspoon Worcestershire sauce
1 teaspoon mustard
1 egg

Put crab meat into a large bowl. Pick out shells, if any. Add seasoning, saltines and parsley. In a separate small bowl, mix mayonnaise, Worcestershire, mustard and egg. Add to crab meat mixture and blend well. Shape into crab cakes. Fry to a golden brown or broil 2 minutes on each side.
Serves: 5 (2-ounce cakes per serving)

Favorite recipe of: Charles A. Castrenze, Owner, Windy Hill Farm,
          Port Deposit, Maryland
Career Highlights: A chef for 26 years, Castrenze has catered hundreds of parties
          where racing fans have enjoyed his crab cakes and crab balls.

RANDY'S REDFISH SAUCE PIQUANT

6 redfish fillets
1 small onion, chopped
1 small bell pepper, chopped
1 bunch green onions, chopped (reserve some for garnish)
4-5 cloves garlic, chopped
1 large can tomato sauce
½ cup butter
Salt, red and black pepper to taste
Garlic powder to taste
1 pound lump crab meat

Saute vegetables in large pan with butter. When wilted, add tomato sauce and stir. Add seasoned fillets. Spoon sauce on top, cover and cook over low heat. Never stir or fish will break, just spoon around fish and shake the pan. When fish has cooked about 5 minutes, add crab meat to top of each fillet. Again spoon sauce over crab meat. Garnish with chopped green onion tops, cover and cook over low heat until well heated. Serve over rice.
Serves: 6

Favorite recipe of: Randy Romero, Jockey, New Orleans, Louisiana
Career Highlights: One of only two jockeys (Terry Lipham is the other) to ride
in both the Kentucky Derby and the All-American Futurity; only rider
to win titles at all five Louisiana racetracks; won riding titles
at Keeneland (twice) and Churchill Downs in Kentucky and
Arlington Park (1982), setting a record for wins at the Chicago track.

TROUT SMILIE

4 6-8 ounce trout fillets
Salt and pepper to taste
½ cup butter, melted
Italian bread crumbs
4 ounces lump crab meat
1 bunch green onion, chopped
Juice of 2 lemons
White wine

Salt and pepper trout fillets and set aside. Coat the bottom of a baking pan with ¼ of the melted butter. Sprinkle bread crumbs in pan and lay fillets on top. Coat fish with butter and sprinkle with bread crumbs to coat fish. Place 1 ounce of crab meat on top of each fillet. Add chopped green onions all over crab meat and fish. Douse with butter and lemon juice and bake at 400° for about 15 minutes. Just before removing from oven, give each fish a little hit of wine.
Serves: 4

Favorite recipe of: Rodney Salvaggio, Owner, Smilie's Restaurant, Harahan, Louisiana
Racing interest: Thoroughbred owner with father, Ben Salvaggio.

SHAUGHNESSY'S TROUT

"Quick and delicious microwave trout recipe"

6 trout fillets
1 can taco sauce
6 slices mozzarella cheese

Cover each fillet with sauce in a pyrex baking dish. Cover with plastic wrap and microwave on high for 9 minutes. Uncover and place a slice of cheese on each fillet. Recover and heat for 1 minute. DO NOT SALT FISH.
Serves; 6

Origin: Terry P. Shaughnessy, Catch and Kill Club, Hackberry, Louisiana
    "After our group caught over 200 Speckled Trout in one morning, Terry
    suggested this recipe. It's so easy and so good!"
Favorite recipe of: J. J. Pletcher, Trainer, Benton, Louisiana
Career Highlights: In 1978, won the Goldrush Futurity and the Land of Enchantment
    Futurity with *Nativo Rango* and the New Mexico Futurity
    with *Hondo Leader.*

CHEF MOSCA'S TROUT MEUNIERE

4 4-ounce fillets of trout or substitute sole or flounder
½ teaspoon salt
2 tablespoons flour
6 tablespoons butter, divided
2 tablespoons fresh lemon juice
1 tablespoons Worcestershire sauce

Sprinkle fish with salt; dredge in flour. In large skillet melt 2 tablespoons butter. Add trout; saute over moderate heat until golden, about 2 minutes on each side. Remove to a platter and keep warm. In a small skillet melt remaining butter. Add lemon juice and Worcestershire. Simmer until thoroughly heated, about 2 minutes. Pour over fish. Garnish with lemon wedges and parsley, if desired.
Serve: 2-4

Favorite recipe of: Chef Nick Mosca, Owner, Lenfant's Restaurant,
    New Orleans, Louisiana

MARYDEL'S BROILED FISH FILLETS

Fish fillets (use your favorite)
Mayonnaise

Cover fish with a light coat of mayonnaise and broil until done, depending on thickness of fish. Mayonnaise will turn brown. Needs no basting. Delicious with sole, yellowtail, red snapper, grouper, dolphin, etc. Gives fish a mild lemony taste.
Serves: As many as desired

Favorite recipe of: Mary R. Odom, Marydel Farm, Middletown, Delaware

SPOTTED CATFISH ETOUFFEE

5-10 pounds spotted catfish, cut in large pieces (Fresh water catfish)
1 tablespoon red cayenne pepper
Salt and pepper to taste
3 tablespoons salad oil
1 large onion, chopped
2 cloves garlic, chopped fine
½ cup extra-fine flour
1 8-ounce can tomato sauce
1 8-ounce can water

Season fish with cayenne, salt and pepper. Add oil to a large black iron pot that you can handle well enough to shake. Add seasoned fish, onions, garlic and sprinkle with flour. Pour tomato sauce and water over all and heat over medium heat. Do not stir fish while cooking; just shake the pot occasionally. Cook until tender, about 30-40 minutes. Serve over rice.
Serves: 6-8

Favorite recipe of: J. Y. Soileau, Trainer, Velle Platte, Louisiana
Career Highlights: Training for about 18 years, started with Quarter horses in match races; trained such stake winners as, *Daring Jester, Ray's Law, Clayhill, Bidabunch* and *Boy's Nite Out* (now at stud); owner of Thoroughbred farm in Ville Platte where he breeds a few mares; Has promising three-year-old Louisiana-bred filly, *Little Biddy Comet.*

FLOUNDER FLORENTINE

4 skinless founder fillets
1½ cups boiling water
10-ounce package frozen chopped spinach
1 tablespoon finely chopped onion
½ teaspoon marjoram
2 tablespoons flour
1 cup skim milk
½ teaspoon salt
Dash pepper
2 tablespoons grated Parmesan cheese

Place fish fillets in 1 cup boiling water. Cook, uncovered, 2 minutes. Drain. Place spinach and onion in ½ cup boiling water. Separate spinach with fork, When water returns to boiling, cover and cook spinach about 2 minutes. Drain well and mix with marjoram. Put spinach in 8x8x12-inch glass baking dish. Arrange cooked fish on top of spinach. Mix flour thoroughly with ¼ cup of milk. Pour remaining milk in sauce pan and heat. Add flour mixture slowly to hot milk, stirring constantly. Cook until thickened. Stir in salt and pepper. Pour over fish. Sprinkle with Parmesan cheese and bake at 400° until top is lightly browned and mixture is bubbly, about 25 minutes.
Serves: 4

Origin: *The I Love America Diet* by Phyllis George and Bill Adler
Favorite recipe of: Phyllis George Brown, Co-host, CBS Morning News
Career Highlights: Former Miss America; worked on CBS Sports' "NFL Today" show;
                    former first lady of Kentucky as the wife of former Governor
                    John Y. Brown.

TUNA SPINACH AU GRATIN

1 7-ounce can tuna, drained and flaked
⅓ cup fine dry bread crumbs
1 10-ounce package frozen chopped spinach, cooked and drained
1 tablespoon lemon juice
2 tablespoons grated Parmesan cheese
¼ teaspoon salt and pepper
½ cup mayonnaise
Chopped black olives

Blend the first 6 ingredients. Add chopped olives and fold in mayonnaise. Spoon into individual shells, 9-inch pie plate or small casserole. Sprinkle with additional cheese. Bake for 20 minutes at 350°. This recipe may be doubled or tripled easily.
Serves: 4

Favorite recipe of: Mr. and Mrs. William I. Levy, Owners, Bay Harbor Farm,
                    Versailles, Kentucky

KINGDOM COME

4 ducks (or 2 geese)
Celery
2 apples
2 cans consomme
1 can water
Cooked and crumbled bacon
SAUCE:
1½ cups butter
½ cup bourbon
5 ounces currant jelly
4 tablespoons Worcestershire sauce
⅔ cup sherry
Flour, if necessary

Stuff birds with celery and apple. Place breast side down in consomme and water. Cover tightly and cook for 3 hours at 350° Cool. Slice meat off carcass. Place duck on mound of rice and spoon on a little sauce. Sprinkle with bacon. Pass sauce with platter.
Sauce: Slowly heat all sauce ingredients in saucepan. Thicken with flour if too thin.
Serves: 6-8

Origin: Stephens, Inc., Little Rock, Arkansas
Favorite recipe of: Mr. & Mrs. J. C. Pohlhaus, Sherwood Manor Farm,
Claiborne, Maryland
Racing interest: Still trying in the breeding end of the business. "If you can chew your losing tickets. I'm sure they would be palatable with this sauce."
Jessie M. Pohlhaus

BROOKS BARBECUED QUAIL

Quail breasts, or quail with leg portions attached
Jalapeno peppers, sliced (fresh jalapeno should be cooked first)
Onion, chopped
Garlic powder
Black pepper
Bacon, thick sliced is preferrable

Clean quail and pat dry with paper towel. Season with garlic powder and pepper. Stuff with a few slices of jalapeno peppers and chopped onion. Wrap each quail breast in bacon. With the thick sliced bacon you are able to stretch 1 slice to cover the whole quail. Cook on a slow barbecue grill for 45 minutes to 1 hour. Optional: Fresh mushrooms may be added to stuffing if desired.
Serves: As many as desired

Original recipe of: Mrs. Louis (Charlotte) Brooks, Jr.,
Thoroughbred Owner, Sweetwater, Texas

WILD DUCKS

2 large mallards
Salt and medium grind pepper
1 large onion, quartered
Kitchen Bouquet

Wash and dry ducks. Rub inside cavity with generous amount of salt, pepper and Kitchen Bouquet. Stuff with onion and rub outside with generous amount of salt, pepper and Kitchen Bouquet. Place ducks in roasting pan and cover tightly. Bake at 325° for 3½-4 hours (or until meat is tender). Cut meat from bone, place in shallow dish and pour sauce from pan over meat. Easy but oh so good!
Serves: 3-4

Favorite recipe of: Amelda L. Wiggins, Thoroughbred Racing Fan,
Haughton, Louisiana

DRAW AWAY DUCK RECIPE

3 ducks (Mallards)
3 large onions, finely chopped
1 cup butter
2 cloves garlic, finely chopped
1 cup Burgundy wine
1½ tablespoons flour
Water
Salt and pepper to taste

Salt and pepper ducks and brown in iron pot. Brown well. Make a roux: Take ducks out of pot, put in flour and stir into remaining butter in pot. Continue stirring constantly until roux is thick and brown. Add onions and continue stirring over low heat. Cook onions until tender. Add 1½ cups water and garlic. Return ducks to pot and simmer over low heat, adding water as needed. Add wine the last 30 minutes of cooking time and baste often. Cook until ducks are tender and gravy is very thick, approximately 5-6 hours.
Serves: 2-3

Origin: Jerry Waters, Hawkeye Hunting Club, Center, Texas
"Hint on cooking game: Game can be overcooked 2-3 hours with no change in quality. However, it can be ruined by undercooking as little as 5 minutes.
Because game has a tendency to be dry, always serve with gravy or light sauce."
Favorite recipe of: Jane Winegardner, Thoroughbred Owner, Louisville, Kentucky

"Draw away — To Win going away; 'draw clear'; 'draw out'."

HIGH FLYER

12 quail
3 lemons, quartered
8-10 slices slightly stale bread
1 small onion, chopped
1 stalk celery, chopped
White wine
1 apple, chopped
½ cup raisins
1 stick butter
Salt, pepper, paprika and poultry seasoning, to taste
12 slices bacon, uncooked

Wash quail in warm water and pat dry. Squeeze lemon quarter on inside of each bird. Set aside. In medium size bowl, crumble bread and mix with chopped apple, raisins and seasonings. In saucepan, heat butter, chopped onion and celery over low heat for about 5 minutes, then mix in with dry ingredients. Use this mixture to stuff each bird, then wrap each bird in a slice of bacon. Place breast side up in 8 x 12-inch pyrex dish. Season slightly and pour about 1 inch of white wine into dish. Cook at 325° for 1 hour.
Serves: 6

Favorite recipe of: Helen C. Alexander, Owner/Breeder, Lexington, Kentucky
Career Highlights: "Biggest Thrill — *Althea;* Career High — (to date) being breeder of two champions in one year and topping Fasig-Tipton Summer Sale in same year!"

QUAIL VERONIQUE

2 dressed and stuffed quail
Melted butter for basting
½ carrot, minced
½ onion, minced
½ celery stalk, minced
Pinch thyme
1 glass dry white wine
½ cup chicken broth
Blend of 2 parts butter and 1 part flour
Chopped fresh parsley

Put dressed and stuffed quail in 450° oven, basting with butter often for 20-25 minutes. Remove birds from the pan, add carrot, onion, celery and thyme to the juice in the pan. Simmer this mixture until it turns light brown. Stir in wine and chicken broth. Thicken liquid with blend of butter and flour. Stir sauce until it is smooth and then spoon over birds. Sprinkle with chopped parsley.
Serves: 1

Favorite recipe of: Bennett Parke, Director of Racing Detroit Race Course, Livonia, Michigan

VENISON STEW

2 pounds venison, cut in 1-inch cubes
4 tablespoons bacon drippings
Water
1 teaspoon garlic salt
1 teaspoon Worcestershire sauce
1½ teaspoon salt
½ teaspoon black pepper
Dash red pepper
¾ cup chopped onion
4 medium potatoes, quartered
6 medium carrots, sliced
1 green pepper, chopped
2 cups sliced celery
3 tablespoons all purpose flour
¼ cup cold water

Brown venison cubes in hot bacon drippings in heavy dutch oven. Add water to cover and seasonings and onion. Cover and simmer about 2 hours. Add potatoes, carrots, pepper and celery and cook about 20 minutes or until vegetables are tender. Taste and adjust seasonings. Dissolve flour in ¼ cup cold water and stir into stew. Cook about 5 minutes.
Serves: 8

Origin: Since Tony hunts so often, his wife, Nancy is always looking for different ways
        to prepare game. She found this recipe in a hunting magazine.
Favorite recipe of: Tony Foyt, Trainer, Louisville, Kentucky

WILD AGAIN
(Wild Rabbit)

1 2-pound rabbit
2 tablespoons vinegar
1 clove garlic, chopped
1 small onion, chopped
½ medium bell pepper, chopped
1 sweet red pepper, chopped
1 hot pepper, chopped
Cooking oil, enough to cover bottom of deep skillet
2 medium onions, chopped

Mix first 5 chopped vegetables with vinegar. Make slits on meaty parts of rabbit and stuff with vegetable seasonings. Add oil to a deep skillet and place on medium heat. When oil is hot, add rabbit and brown on all sides. (If rabbit sticks, add a few tablespoons of water. When rabbit is browned, add additional onions and saute until onions are browned. Don't be afraid to burn onions, the darker the onions, the better the sauce. Add two cups of water and cook until gravy thickens.
If rabbit is tough, cover skillet after adding water and let cook for about 15 minutes or until rabbit is tender. More water may be necessary. Uncover and simmer 10 minutes.
Larger rabbit may require longer cooking time.
Serve rabbit over rice with gravy. This dish is delicious with salad and hot French bread.
Serves: 2-4

Origin: Barbara Duplechin (Pat Day's sister-in-law), Lafayette, Louisiana
       This recipe was sent to Pat and *Wild Again* with a message from
       Barbara, "Thanks for the thrill!"
Favorite recipe of: Pat Day, Jockey, Arlington Heights, Illinois
Career Highlights: Rider who guided *Wild Again* to victory in the Inaugural
       Breeder's Cup Classic. Pat was also honored with the Eclipse Award
       for leading rider in the country in races won in 1983 and 1984.

"Rate — To restrain a horse early in race, conserving its energies for later challenges."

FRIED OYSTER SANDWICH

16 fresh oysters, shucked and drained
½ cup all purpose flour
½ cup fine bread crumbs
1 egg
1 tablespoon light cream
Generous sprinkling white pepper
4 tablespoons butter
8 slices thick white bread, toasted
2 tablespoons butter
8 slices thick bacon, cooked crisp
4 leaves lettuce
12 dashes Tabasco
8 twists fresh ground pepper

Drain oysters, pat dry with paper towel. Mix flour and bread crumbs. Beat egg with cream and pepper in a bowl. Roll oysters in flour mixture, then in egg, then again in flour. Heat a large skillet over medium heat and add butter. When sizzling, fry oysters until browned, turn and brown other side. Drain on paper towels. Toast bread, butter 1 side of each slice. Assemble by adding 1 leaf lettuce, 2 strips bacon and 4 oysters to each sandwich. Add 3 dashes Tabasco, 2 twists of pepper and top with remaining slice of bread.
Yield: 4 sandwiches

Origin: Recipe for frying oysters — "The Grand Central Oyster Bar and Restaurant
　　　　Seafood Cook Book" by Jerome Brody. Otherwise, sandwich is original.
Favorite recipe of: Dr. Ronald E. Waggener, Thoroughbred Owner, Omaha, Nebraska

HOT HAM SANDWICHES

3 pounds shaved ham
1½ pounds shaved Swiss cheese
½ pound butter, softened
2 tablespoons poppy seed
5 tablespoons yellow mustard
1 large onion, cut in chunks
12 large hamburger buns

Mix butter, poppy seed, mustard and onion in blender. Spread inside of hamburger buns with blender mixture and add shaved ham and top with shaved cheese. Wrap each bun in foil and heat in oven for 20 minutes in 350° oven. If using a microwave, wrap in plastic wrap and heat for 1-1½ minutes. These can be made and put in freezer and used whenever you want a good sandwich. Do not bake before freezing.
Yield: 12 sandwiches

Favorite recipe of: Steve and Mary Jo Gasper, Omaha, Nebraska
Career Highlights:　Raising, breeding and training horses at Walmac
　　　　　　　　　　Farm in Lexington, Kentucky.

Stretch Run

Vegetables

Sauces

Preserves

ASPARAGUS CASSEROLE

4-6 hard boiled eggs
1-2 cans asparagus tips, or chopped asparagus
1 small jar chopped pimentos
½ small onion, sliced
¼ pound cooked spaghetti
2 tablespoon butter
2 tablespoons flour
2 cups milk
1 cup shredded cheese
Dash salt and pepper
Topping: Butter, shredded cheese and bread crumbs

Layer eggs, asparagus, pimentos, onion and spaghetti in greased casserole dish. Make sauce by melting butter in a double boiler and stirring in flour. Add milk and stir until slightly thickened. Add cheese and seasonings and stir until thick. Pour sauce over layers in casserole. Top with slivers of butter, cheese, and bread crumbs (or cracker crumbs). Bake at 350° for 30 minutes.
Serves: 6-8

Favorite recipe of: Mr. & Mrs. Eddie Reynolds, Owner-Manager
Hillside Farm, Paris, Kentucky

GREEN BEANS HORSERADISH

2 cans chicken broth
2 16-ounce cans green beans
1 large onion, chopped
Several pieces ham, chopped
1 cup mayonnaise
1 heaping tablespoon horseradish
1 teaspoon Worcestershire sauce
¼ teaspoon salt
¼ teaspoon garlic salt
¼ teaspoon celery salt
Juice of 1 lemon

Cook beans in broth with onion and ham slowly for 1 hour. Blend mayonnaise with remaining ingredients, set aside at room temperature. When beans are ready to serve, drain and spoon mayonnaise mixture over all. These are good leftover cold or can be stuffed in tomatoes for salad.
Serves: 8

Favorite recipe of: John Ed Anthony, Fordyce, Arkansas
Career Highlights: Owner of *Temperence Hill,* winner of the Belmont Stakes,
Travers, Jockey Gold Cup, Super Derby and Eclipse Award in 1980.

STRING BEANS AND BACON

Fresh green beans
Sliced bacon

Clean beans and cut off ends. Steam until crisp-tender stage, about 10 minutes. Remove from pan and cool. Take about 6 green beans and wrap with a slice of bacon; secure with toothpick. In a skillet, fry each "bundle" until bacon is done.
Serves: As many as desired

Origin: Pamela J. Fitzgerald
Favorite recipe of: Frank L. Brothers, Trainer, New Orleans, Louisiana
Career Highlights: Leading trainer at the Fair Grounds in four of the six seasons between 1978 and 1984; won the 1984 Fair Grounds Classic with *Police Inspector;* won the 1985 New Orleans Handicap with *Westheimer* for his second graded stakes win.

BOSTON BAKED BEANS

2 pounds, dried pea beans or yellow eye beans
1 teaspoon soda
¾ pound salt pork, divided
1 medium onion, thinly sliced
⅔ cup molasses
½ cup sugar
1½ teaspoon dry mustard
2 teaspoons salt
½ teaspoon pepper

Cover beans with water and let soak overnight. In the morning pour off water, cover with fresh water. Add soda and bring slowly to a boil. Simmer 20 minutes, then drain, reserving liquid. Cut half of the salt pork into 1-inch cubes. Place in bottom of a 4-quart bean pot or casserole. Add onion and beans. Mix molasses, sugar, mustard, salt, papper and 2 cups reserved liquid. Pour over beans. Score remaining pieces of salt pork at ½-inch intervals down to the rind. Push pork down into beans with fat side up until about ½ inch protrudes above beans. Add enough bean liquid to just cover beans. Heat oven to 300° (low). Bake beans covered for 3-4 hours. Add a little hot water as necessary to keep juice bubbling at top of pot during entire baking time.
Serves: 10-12

Origin: Mrs. Tom (Anne) Sweeney's Rhode Island Recipe.
Favorite recipe of: Thomas S. Sweeney, Senior Vice President and General Manager of Louisiana Downs, Bossier City, Louisiana

EDDIE D'S BAKED BEANS

1 pound ground round
2 16-ounce cans pork and beans
1 medium onion, chopped
1 bell pepper, chopped
1 teaspoon salt
1 teaspoon cayenne pepper
½ cup brown sugar
1 tablespoon ketchup
1 tablespoon mustard
2 tablespoons barbecue sauce
Bacon slices for garnish

Brown ground round. Add onions and bell pepper and cook until tender. Mix beans, seasonings, sugar, ketchup, mustard and barbecue sauce in a casserole. Add meat mixture to casserole and stir. Put slices of bacon on top and bake covered at 300° for 20 minutes. Remove cover and bake an additional 10 minutes.
Serves: 6

Origin: Mrs. Eddie (Juanita) Delahoussaye's Family
Favorite recipe of: Eddie Delahousaye, Jockey, Arcadia, California
Career Highlights: Rider of the 1982 and 1983 Kentucky Derby winners, *Gato del Sol* and *Sunny's Halo.*

BACKSIDE BARBECUED BEANS

1 pound bacon, cut in thirds
2 medium onions, chopped
½ cup bell pepper, chopped
5 15-ounce cans pork and beans
1½ cups ketchup
1 package brown sugar (2½ cups)
¼ cup prepared mustard
¼ cup Worcestershire sauce
2 teaspoons liquid smoke

Fry bacon in 4-quart pot until crisp. Add onions and bell pepper and saute until clear. Add beans and remaining ingredients. Stir well and cook uncovered. Simmer until cooked down to desired consistency, about 1-2 hours.
Serves: 20

Favorite recipe of: D. L. Butler, Shreveport, Louisiana
Racing interests: D. L. Butler is a Certified Public Accountant who handles the taxes and financial affairs of many leading jockeys, trainers and other race track personnel. He and his wife, Midgie, are very popular race track enthusiasts who travel to the Fair Grounds, Oaklawn Park, Louisiana Downs or wherever the races take them.

"Backside — The area usually behind or next to the racetrack where the horses are stabled."

FRED'S REDS

2 pounds dried Louisiana red kidney beans
2 large onions, finely chopped
4-6 ham steaks, cut into chunks or 1½-2 pounds baked ham
1 pound sliced bacon
1½ pounds smoked beef sausage, cut into bite-size pieces
Pepper to taste
Louisiana hot sauce, to taste

Combine onions and beans in a large pot. Cover with water approximately 4-6 inches over the level of the beans and onions. Soak overnight. The following day, bring the mixture to a boil. Add ham and bacon. Reduce to a simmer and allow the mixture to cook all day, stirring frequently to prevent sticking. (If for some reason you have to leave, simply turn the beans off and upon returning, continue simmering.) Allow the mixture to cook as long as possible the first day. The following morning, continue to simmer the beans. Put the smoked sausage pieces under the broiler for 3-5 minutes or until lightly browned. Add the sausage and the drippings to the bean mixture. Continue cooking until evening meal. Serve over rice.
Serves: 12-15 hungry people

Favorite recipe of: Fred Aime, Jockey Agent, New Orleans, Louisiana
Career Highlights: Currently handling the riding engagements of Randy Romero. Handled Eddie Delahoussaye in 1978, the year he was leading rider in the country. Fred's wide ranging experience in the various aspects of Thoroughbred racing has contributed to his success as a jockey agent. The success of his red beans can be attributed to the tried and true methods described above. Fred's Reds are a favorite among racetrackers especially at the Fair Grounds in New Orleans.

BETSY'S PICKLED CARROTS

2 pounds carrots, pared and sliced
½ cup chopped green pepper
1 3½-ounce jar cocktail onions, drained
1 10½-ounce can tomato soup
¼ teaspoon pepper
1 teaspoon Worcestershire sauce
1 cup sugar
¾ cup wine vinegar
½ cup salad oil
1 teaspoon salt
1 teaspoon dry mustard

Cook carrots in boiling water until just tender. Drain and cool. Combine carrots, green pepper and onion in bowl. Mix remaining ingredients. Pour over vegetables. Cover and refrigerate 2 DAYS. Drain and serve cold. "Great to make ahead for a party."
Serves: 10

Origin: Mrs. David E. (Betsy) Hager, II
Favorite recipe of: David E. Hager, II, Manager, Idle Hour Farm, Paris Kentucky

CARROTS AND PARSNIPS A LA SHOEMAKER

3 carrots, peeled and sliced
3 parsnips, peeled and sliced
2 tablespoons honey
2 tablespoons cinnamon

Boil or steam carrots and parsnips to desired tenderness. Drain and add honey and sprinkle with cinnamon. Stir to mix and serve. "Really tasty, try it!"
Serves: 3

Favorite recipe of: William Shoemaker, Jockey, San Marino, California
Career Highlights: To say that Shoemaker is the greatest jockey of all time is obvious
but obligatory. In his 36 years of race riding, he has led the
continent in annual wins and earnings more times than
any other rider.

STUFFED BELL PEPPERS

6 bell peppers
2 large onions, finely chopped
1 bunch green onions, chopped
2-3 stalks celery, chopped
4 tablespoons margarine
½ pound ground beef or shrimp
1 clove garlic, finely minced
1½ cups Italian bread crumbs
4-5 inch piece French bread, soaked in about ½ cup water
1 egg
3 tablespoons cream
Salt, pepper, parsley and basil, to taste

Cut peppers in half lengthwise. Remove seeds and membrane. Drop into boiling water. Parboil 5 minutes. Rinse in cold water and set aside. Saute onions, green onions and celery in margarine until tender. Add shrimp or beef, and garlic. Cook over low heat until meat browns, if using beef. Add bread crumbs and bread soaked in water. Blend well and remove from heat. Beat egg and cream until fluffy and quickly stir into mixture. Add remaining seasonings and mix thoroughly. Fill pepper shells with mixture. Place peppers in a shallow 9x13-inch baking pan with a small amount of water at the bottom. Bake in a preheated 350° oven for 15-20 minutes. Tops of stuffed peppers may be sprinkled with bread crumbs or Parmesan cheese before baking, if desired.
Serves: 6

Origin: Joy Cobena, Metairie, Louisiana
Favorite recipe of: The Editor

BROCCOLI-HAM ROLLUPS

1 bunch fresh broccoli or 2 packages frozen broccoli spears
2 tablespoons butter or margarine
2 tablespoons flour
¼ teaspoon salt
½ teaspoon dry mustard
1 cup milk
1 cup (4 ounces) Sharp Cheddar cheese, finely shredded
6 slices boiled ham, thinly sliced and about 6 inches, 1 ounce each

Preheat oven to 350° (moderate). Cook broccoli until just tender. Melt butter in a heavy saucepan. Stir in flour, salt and mustard. Gradually stir in milk. Cook, stirring constantly, until thickened. Add cheese and continue stirring until cheese is melted. Do not overcook. Divide broccoli spears into 6 portions, splitting large stalks as necessary. Alternate directions of flower ends within each portion. Place broccoli on ham and roll as for jellyroll with broccoli in the center of each rollup. Arrange in baking dish with seam side down. Pour sauce over rollups and bake until sauce is bubbly, about 20 minutes.
Variation: Asparagus-Ham Rollups — Substitute asparagus for broccoli.
Serves: 6

Favorite recipe of: Phyllis George Brown, Co-host CBS Morning News
Career Highlights: A former Miss America; a network television personality, an Emmy
　　　　　　　　　 Award winner the mother of Lincoln Tyler George Brown and
　　　　　　　　　 married to former Kentucky Governor John Y. Brown, Jr.

BROCCOLI CASSEROLE

¼ cup chopped celery
¼ cup chopped onion
3 tablespoons butter
½ cup milk
2 cups cooked rice
1 8-ounce jar cheese spread, melted
1 can cream of chicken soup
1 can water chestnuts, drained and chopped
1 pound fresh broccoli, cooked and chopped
Shredded sharp cheese for topping

Saute celery and onion in butter. Add milk and mix in rice, cheese spread, soup, water chestnuts and broccoli. Season to taste. Put in casserole dish and top with shredded cheese. Bake at 250° for 20-30 minutes.
Serves: 4-6

Origin: Mrs. Larry (Jeanette) Snyder
Favorite recipe of: Larry Snyder, Jockey, Hot Springs, Arkansas
Career Highlights: Hall of Fame rider who has won over 5,000 races; won a record 150
　　　　　　　　　 races during the 1984 Louisiana Downs meeting to record his
　　　　　　　　　 fourth straight riding title; led the nation in victories with 352 in
　　　　　　　　　 1969; leading rider at Oaklawn Park seven times, including three
　　　　　　　　　 straight between 1980 and 1982.

CREAMED CAULIFLOWER CASSEROLE

1 medium head cauliflower
3 tablespoons butter or margarine
¼ cup flour
2 cups milk
¾ teaspoon salt
⅛ teaspoon pepper
2 cups herb seasoned stuffing
¾ cup water
½ cup butter or margarine, melted

Break cauliflower into small pieces and cook until just tender. Drain and place in a shallow 2-quart casserole. Melt 3 tablespoons butter or margarine in a medium saucepan. Stir in flour and cook a few minutes while stirring. Remove from heat and blend in milk. Bring to a boil, stirring constantly, and simmer until thickened. Season to taste and pour over cauliflower in casserole. Combine the last 3 ingredients and spoon over top. Bake at 350° for 30 minutes.
Variation: Broccoli used in place of cauliflower makes a delicious change.
Serves: 6-8

Favorite recipe of: Steve and Mary Jo Gasper, Omaha, Nebraska
Career Highlights: Lived in Lexington, Kentucky on Walmac Farm, boarding and raising
                     thoroughbreds. Son, John J. Gasper, works as a Jockey Agent.

SOLID PERFORMER
(Corn and Broccoli Casserole)

1 can creamed corn
1 package frozen chopped broccoli, cooked and drained
1 egg, beaten
½ cup cracker crumbs (12 crackers)
¼ cup chopped onion
Salt and pepper to taste
2 tablespoons margarine

Mix corn, broccoli, egg and onion gently. Season with salt and pepper to taste and pour into a 1-quart greased casserole. Sprinkle with cracker crumbs and dot with margarine. Bake at 350° for 35-40 minutes.
Serves: 4

Favorite recipe of: Virginia S. DeWitt, Trainer, Hollywood, Florida
Career Highlights: "When *Solo Lady* broke her maiden and beat colts in Ohio in 1978;
                    when a filly my husband trained beat *Stymie* in the Suburban
                    Handicap in 1948.

"Solid Performer — Of a ready horse, suitably placed."

LUCILLE'S EASY DISH-KENTUCKY STYLE
(Corn Pudding)

1 egg
1½ tablespoon flour
1½ tablespoon sugar
½ cup milk
1 16-ounce can cream style corn
2 tablespoons butter

Mix egg, flour and sugar. When well blended, add milk and corn. Pour into a greased casserole, dot with butter, and bake in 350° oven for about 1 hour. Test for doneness by inserting a knife into middle. If knife comes out clean, its done.
Serves: 4

Origin: Mrs. Woody (Lucille) Stephens
Favorite recipe of: W. C. (Woody) Stephens, Trainer, Long Island, New York
Career Highlights: Woody's "biggest thrill" in his remarkable career as a trainer has been winning *four* consecutive Belmont Stakes with *Conquistador Cielo* (1982), *Caveat* (1983), *Swale* (1984) and *Creme Fraiche* (1985).

CHILE CORN PUDDING

1 10-ounce can whole green chilies
1 16-ounce can cream style corn
1 tablespoon flour
2 eggs, well beaten
¼ cup butter, melted
⅓ cup milk
½ teaspoon salt
Pepper and savory salt to taste
Shredded cheese

Split chilies and line bottom of greased pyrex baking dish. Mix other ingredients (except cheese) and cover chilies. Cover generously with cheese. Bake for 30 minutes or until set at 350°.
Serves: 4

Origin: *Seasoned With Sun,* by the Junior League of El Paso, Inc.
Favorite recipe of: Margaret Varner Bloss, El Paso, Texas
Career Highlights: Only woman to represent the United States in three racket sports: Tennis, Badminton, and Squash Racquets. Owner-Breeder with Margaret duPont of *Net Effect,* 1984 Land of Enchantment winner.

"Consolation double — When horse is scratched from second race after daily-double betting begins, money is set aside to pay those who have bought tickets pairing horse with winner of first race."

CORN CASSEROLE

2 tablespoons butter
1 medium onion, chopped
¼ bell pepper, chopped
2 green onions, chopped (optional)
1 rib celery, chopped
1 can white shoe peg corn
Salt and pepper to taste
2 cans hot tamales, sliced
Chili powder

Saute onions, bell pepper and celery in butter. Add corn and cook slowly a few minutes, stirring frequently. Add salt and pepper to taste. Arrange mixture in a 1½ quart casserole, alternating layers of corn and sliced hot tamales. Sprinkle each layer with chili powder. Bake in 350° oven until thoroughly heated, about 30 minutes. Can be prepared early, refrigerated and baked when ready to serve. Good served with barbecue.
Serves: 4

Origin: Mrs. D. L. (Midgie) Butler
Favorite recipe of: D. L. Butler, Shreveport, Louisiana
Racing interests: D. L. Butler is a Certified Public Accountant who handles the taxes and financial affairs of many well-known jockeys, trainers and other racetrack personnel.

MICROWAVE MACQUE-CHOUX

1 17-ounce can creamed corn
1 17-ounce can kernel corn, drained
1 can Rotel tomatoes
1 teaspoon sugar
1 dash Accent
1 dash pepper

Mix above ingredients in a covered dish and microwave on slow for 15 minutes. Stir at intervals. Cook until hot. Time will vary on microwave used.
Serves: 6-8

Favorite recipe of: Gene Norman, Trainer, Bossier City, Louisiana

VERY EASY EGGPLANT PARMIGIANA

1 medium eggplant, peeled and cut in ½-inch slices
2 cloves garlic, finely minced
1 small onion, finely minced
¼ cup butter
8-ounce can tomato sauce, with chunks of onion, pepper, etc.
½ cup grated Parmesan cheese
¾-1 cup shredded mozzarella cheese

Melt butter in skillet and add garlic and onion. Place eggplant slices in skillet until each has absorbed butter mixture on both sides. Place eggplant on greased cookie sheet under broiler for 5 minutes, turn and broil 2 minutes longer. Transfer to baking dish. Spread with tomato sauce and sprinkle generously with Parmesan cheese. Top with mozzarella. Broil until lightly brown and bubbly, about 5 minutes. Can be made ahead and refrigerated until ready to cook.
Serves: 6

Origin: 1961 New York Times Cook Book
Favorite recipe of: Sam and Jill Maple, Owners, Barefoot Farm, Hot Springs, Arkansas
Career Highlights: Sam remembers riding six stakes winners in a row (including 4 derbies) in the summer of 1979 with *Smarten,* trained by Woody Stephens, owned by Mr. & Mrs. Bob Kirkham. The Derbies were Ohio, Penn, American and Illinois, also finished second by a nose in the Arkansas Derby.

EGGPLANT RICE

1 eggplant, peeled and diced
½ cup chopped onion
1 teaspoon minced garlic
1 tablespoon butter
½ cup fresh, chopped tomatoes
1 bay leaf
½ teaspoon thyme
1 tablespoon minced parsley
½ cup raw rice
1 cup chicken broth
Salt and pepper to taste

Saute onion and garlic in butter until wilted. Add diced eggplant, tomatoes, bay leaf, thyme and parsley. Cook, stirring, for 5 minutes. Add rice, broth and seasonings. Cover and let simmer for 20 minutes. Reheats well in microwave oven.
Serves: 4

Favorite recipe of: Carole Roussel Campo, New Orleans, Louisiana
Career Highlights: Owned *Beau Rit,* winner of Hits Parade Derby at the Fair Grounds and ran in the 1981 Kentucky Derby. Total earnings over $175,000 and still winning!

EGGPLANT CASSEROLE

1 large or 2 small eggplants
1 large onion, chopped
1 bell pepper, chopped
3 tablespoons butter
4 slices bread
½ cup milk
3 eggs, beaten
Salt and pepper to taste
Paprika
8 ounces Cheddar cheese, divided ¾ cubed and ¼ shredded for topping

Peel eggplant, cut in chunks, boil until tender, drain and mash. Brown onion and bell pepper in butter. Cube bread and soak in milk. Mix eggplant, onion mixture and bread together. Add eggs and season with salt and pepper. Add cubed cheese and turn into casserole dish. Top with shredded cheese and sprinkle with paprika. Bake at 400° for 25-30 minutes.
Serves: 6

Origin: Mrs. Forrest (Betty) Kaelin
Favorite recipe of: Forrest Kaelin, Trainer, Finchville, Kentucky

A HOT TIP

4 potatoes, cooked, peeled and sliced
6 tablespoons butter, divided
4 green onions, chopped
1 green pepper, chopped
1 tablespoon flour
1 cup milk
2-ounce jar pimentos, drained and chopped
½ roll each, jalapeno cheese, and garlic cheese

In a skillet, saute onions and pepper in 2 tablespoons butter until soft. In a saucepan, melt remaining 4 tablespoons butter and stir in flour. When blended, add milk, stirring until mixture thickens. Add the onion mixture, pimentos and cheese and simmer until cheeses have melted. In a lightly greased baking dish, arrange sliced potatoes. Pour sauce over potatoes and bake at 350° for 45 minutes.
Serves: 6-8

Favorite recipe of: Peggy S. McReynolds, Bedford, Texas
Career Highlights: Owner of multiple stakes winner, *Explosive Wagon.*

CRABMEAT STUFFED POTATOES

6 baking potatoes
1 pound crab meat
1 cup butter
Sour cream
Green onion tops, chopped
Real bacon bits
Light cream
Shredded Cheddar cheese

Bake potatoes as usual. In a skillet, melt ½ cup butter, add onion tops and saute for 1 minute. Add bacon bits and crab meat, toss carefully and set aside. Scoop out potato pulp from baked potatoes. Add butter, sour cream, light cream and some cheese. Mixture should be moist and creamy. Lightly toss crabmeat mixture with potatoes. Fill potato shells with mixture and top with shredded cheese. Bake at 350° until thoroughly heated, about 30 minutes. Great with steaks!
Serves: 6

Origin: Mrs. Gerald (Mona) Romero
Favorite recipe of: Gerald Romero, Trainer, Haughton, Louisiana
Career Highlights: Set an all time record breaking win percentage at Louisiana Downs for 1984 with 30.3%; at age 28, the youngest trainer to do so.

GOURMET POTATOES

6 medium potatoes, cooked, peeled and coarsely grated
2 cups grated Cheddar cheese
6 tablespoons butter, divided
1½ cups sour cream
⅓ cup minced onion
1 teaspoon salt
¼ teaspoon black pepper
Paprika

Melt cheese with 4 tablespoons butter in top of double boiler. Remove from heat and blend in sour cream, onion and seasonings. Fold mixture into potatoes and turn into a buttered 1½-quart shallow baking dish. Dot with remaining 2 tablespoons butter and sprinkle lightly with paprika. Bake at 350° for 30 minutes.
Serves: 6-8

Origin: Chicago Tribune
Favorite recipe of: Thomas S. Sweeney, Senior Vice President and General Manager of Louisiana Downs, Bossier City, Louisiana

POTATO BOLINI

10 medium potatoes
1 large onion
Salt and pepper to taste
3 heaping tablespoons flour
3 eggs, beaten
Oil for frying

Shred potatoes and onion in processor. In a large bowl, mix potatoes with seasonings, flour and eggs. Heat oil (enough to cover bottom) in an iron skillet. When oil is very hot, pick up a handful of potato mixture, allowing excess moisture to drip off, and drop into hot skillet. DO NOT SMASH. When golden brown, turn with spatula and brown other side. Drain on paper towel and serve.
Serves: 6

Favorite recipe of: Jerry Hissam, Jockey Agent, Hot Springs, Arkansas

DOUBLE DIPPED
FRENCH FRIED ONION RINGS

2 eggs
Small amount of milk
Salt and pepper to taste
Pinch of sugar
1 large onion
1 cup flour, more may be needed
Oil for frying

Mix together eggs, milk, salt, pepper and sugar. Put flour into a sturdy brown bag and season with salt, pepper and sugar. Slice onion into ¼-inch slices. Push out each slice into individual rings. Throw away center parts that are not rings. Dip a bunch into the egg and milk batter, shake in bag of flour, dip again into egg batter and again shake in flour. THEY ARE NOW DOUBLE DIPPED. They fry in a few minutes in very hot oil. When golden brown, take out of oil with a fork, let drip and drain on paper towels. Can be lightly salted and put in a 325° oven until ready to serve or serve immediately.
Serves: 4

Origin: Developed by 'Gene Liss, who says, "MAKE PLENTY, they are better than ANY you've ever tasted. They're not greasy and do not cause any stomach growling."
Favorite recipe of: 'Gene Liss, Owner, Missouri Stud
Career Highlights: Missouri's only registered bloodstock agent; owns "absolutely it's best bred stallion, *Toil and Trouble*", 4-year-old son of Lyphard as well as sons of *Explodent*, *Raja Baba* mares, a racing string with a high percentage of firsts and seconds and "the best broodmare band in the mid-west featuring real winning mares in foal to sons of great sires." Next year he promises to reveal his formula for "Half Hour Barbecue Ribs" mellowed in a secret sauce that is smoother and better than any you've ever tasted.

SIDE SADDLE YAMS

1 large can (or more) yams
1 pound bacon, cut in half
½ box wooden toothpicks

Drain yams well. Cut each yam into quarters. Wrap each yam quarter with a half slice of bacon and secure with toothpick. Place in a non-greased 9x13-inch pan and bake at 350° for 25-30 minutes or until bacon is done. Drain on paper towel and serve with any main dish.
Serves: 10

Origin: Mrs. Doris (Alice) Hebert, Abbeville, Louisiana
Favorite recipe of: Doris Hebert, Trainer
Career Highlights: Achieving the title of leading trainer at Jefferson Downs and
                    Evangeline Downs in Louisiana.

TRIPLE CROWN SUPREME

3 cups mashed sweet potatoes
1 cup sugar
4 tablespoons margarine
½ cup milk
1 teaspoon salt
2 eggs
1 teaspoon vanilla
1 cup brown sugar
⅓ cup chopped nuts
⅓ cup flour
3 tablespoons margarine, melted
1 cup coconut

Mix first 7 ingredients together and pour into well greased 1½-quart casserole dish. For topping mix remaining ingredients and sprinkle to cover potatoes. Bake for 30 minutes at 325°.
Serves: 6-8

Favorite recipe of: Julio Espinoza, Jockey, Louisville, Kentucky
Career Highlights: Tied record for leading rider at Churchill Downs four
                    consecutive times.

"Triple Crown — Mythical award to any three-year-old that wins Kentucky Derby, Preakness Stakes and Belmont Stakes."

JEANNE'S GREEN RICE

4 cups cooked rice, hot
½ cup melted butter
½ teaspoon salt
¼ teaspoon Tabasco sauce
3 lightly beaten egg yolks
3 stiffly beaten egg whites
½ cup finely minced fresh parsley
1 cup finely minced green onions, green tops only

Place hot cooked rice (not over cooked in a mixing bowl. Add ¾ of the melted butter and mix well. Add salt and Tabasco and toss. Blend in egg yolks, then the parsley and green onions mixing until rice begins to acquire a rich green color. Add the stiffly beaten egg whites and mix again. Butter a mold or casserole with remaining butter. Pour in ingredients and bake in moderate oven (350°) for 1 hour until firm. Unmold to platter or serve from the casserole dish. Serve with Shrimp Raymond.
Serves: 8

Origin: Chris Blake's Restaurant of the 1960's.
Favorite recipe of: Jeanne S. Salmen, New Orleans, Louisiana
Career Highlights: "Owned and raced many horses with my late husband, Raymond F. Salmen, since we first started in 1969. The greatest horse racing in our colors was *A Letter To Harry* who won numerous stakes all over the country.

RICE A LA PATSY

1 pound fresh mushrooms
2 tablespoons butter
1 cup long grain rice, uncooked
Salt and pepper to taste

Put mushrooms through a grinder and saute in butter. Simmer 15 minutes. Boil rice in 2 cups water for approximately 10 minutes. Rinse in cold water and drain well. Add salt and pepper and mix well with mushrooms. Put into a well buttered 1-quart ring mold. Set mold in a pan of boiling water and bake at 300° for 45 minutes.
Tip: "Put strips of oiled waxed paper in the ring mold before packing in rice for easy removal."
Serves: 6

Origin: Moffat family recipe
Favorite recipe of: Patricia M. Pope, Owner, El Peco Ranch, Medera, California

WILD RICE AND SPINACH CASSEROLE

2 tablespoons butter
1 medium onion, finely chopped
¼ pound fresh sliced mushrooms
1 10-ounce package frozen chopped spinach
1 6-ounce package long grain and wild rice
2 teaspoons Dijon mustard
¼ teaspoon salt
2¼ cups water
1 8-ounce package cream cheese, softened

In a skillet, melt butter, add onion, mushrooms and frozen spinach. Over low heat, cook until spinach is thawed. Stir in rice and seasoning packets, mustard, salt and water. Pour into a two-quart casserole with a lid. Bake covered at 375° for 30 minutes. Uncover and stir in cheese. Return to oven and bake an additional 10 minutes.
Serves: 6-8

Favorite recipe of: The Editor "Delicious with baked cornish hens or Trout Meuniere."

GREEN PHUNQUE
(Pronounced "Funk")

1 10-ounce box cut leaf spinach
½ cup butter, divided
1 medium onion, chopped, divided
4 tablespoons flour
1 cup milk
1 teaspoon sugar
Salt and pepper to taste
¾ cup fresh chopped mushrooms
4 eggs, beaten
1 cup chopped cooked bacon
Cheddar cheese, shredded

Cook spinach according to package directions and drain. In a saucepan, melt 4 tablespoons butter and ¼ onion and saute until clear. Stir in flour and cook to a paste. Add milk and stir until the sauce thickens. Add sugar, salt and pepper, then mix sauce with spinach. Melt remaining butter in saucepan, add remaining onion and saute. Add mushrooms and saute 1 minute. Add eggs, bacon cooking until eggs scramble. Stir in spinach mixture. Transfer to casserole, sprinkle top with cheese. Put under broiler until cheese melts. Serve hot.
Serves: 6-8

Origin: Mrs. Larry (Becky) Melancon
Favorite recipe of: Tony Foyt, Trainer, Louisville, Kentucky

ARKANSAS SPINACH ROCKEFELLER

1 package frozen chopped spinach
½ cup milk
½ cup cubed sharp cheese
Juice of 1 lemon
6 green onions, chopped
2 tablespoons butter
1 teaspoon Louisiana hot sauce
1 teaspoon salt
1 egg, beaten
4 tablespoons Parmesan cheese

Cook spinach and squeeze ALL liquid out. Put in saucepan with all ingredients except egg and Parmesan cheese. Heat until cubed cheese melts. Cool and mix in egg. Fill 1-quart greased casserole. Top with Parmesan cheese and bake for 20 minutes at 350°.
Variations: Good baked in artichoke bottoms or stuffed in tomatoes and baked.
Serves: 4

Origin: Mrs. John Ed (Mary Lynn) Anthony
Favorite recipe of: John Ed Anthony, Fordyce, Arkansas
Career Highlights: Owner of *Cox's Ridge,* winner of eleven stakes his 3-4 year old year.

SQUASH CASSEROLE

1½ pounds yellow squash
1 small jar diced pimento, chopped fine
1 small onion, grated
1 cup sour cream
1 can cream of chicken soup
1 package Jiffy Corn Muffin Mix
½ cup butter or margarine, melted

Slice, cook, drain and mash squash. Add pimento, onion, sour cream and soup. Mix well. Combine corn muffin mix with butter. Use ½ of crumbs to line bottom of 9-inch square casserole. Pour squash mixture over crumbs and top with remaining crumbs. Bake at 350° for 30 minutes or until crusty on top. To double recipe, use 9x13-inch casserole. Can also be frozen, thawed and cooked when you need it.
"You can serve this casserole to non-squash eaters, they'll never know."
Serves: 6

Favorite recipe of: Tommie Juneau, Thoroughbred Owner, Dallas, Texas

SPINACH AND RICOTTA STUFFED SQUASH

8 crookneck or zucchini squash, each about 6 inches long
2 tablespoons butter or margarine
1 small onion, finely chopped
1 clove garlic, minced or pressed
1 10-ounce package frozen chopped spinach, thawed
2 eggs
2 cups (1 pound) ricotta cheese
¼ cup grated Parmesan cheese
1 tablespoon chopped parsley
½ teaspoon each salt, dry basil and oregano leaves
Dash pepper
Tomato sauce, recipe below

Trim ends off squash; cut squash in half lengthwise. With a teaspoon scoop out seeds and part of pulp (save pulp for soup stock), leaving shells ½ inch thick. Steam squash shells over boiling water until crisp-tender, about 5 minutes. Plunge in cold water, drain well and set aside. In a small frying pan over medium heat, melt 1 tablespoon butter. Add onion and garlic and cook, stirring occasionally until onion is limp. Squeeze spinach to remove excess moisture. Add spinach to onion mixture and cook for 1 minute; let cool. In a bowl, combine eggs with ricotta, stirring until well blended. Stir in Parmesan, parsley, salt, basil, oregano, pepper and spinach mixture. Allowing about 3 tablespoons filling per squash, mound filling inside squash shells. Arrange filled shells in shallow baking pans. Melt remaining butter; brush over cut surfaces of squash. If made ahead, cover and refrigerate. Bake, uncovered, in a 350° oven for about 20 minutes (30 minutes, if refrigerated) or until filling is piping hot. While squash is baking, prepare tomato sauce to spoon over squash before serving.
Variation: Instead of topping with Tomato Sauce, can sprinkle with additional Parmesan cheese and bake as usual.

TOMATO SAUCE

1 15-ounce can tomato sauce
2 tablespoon chopped parsley
1 clove garlic, minced
1 teaspoon dry basil
½ teaspoon oregano leaves
Salt and pepper to taste

In a 1-quart pan, simmer all ingredients together for about 5 or 10 minutes. Spoon over stuffed squash before serving.
Serves: 8

Origin: "Sunset Menus & Recipes for Vegetarian Cooking"
Favorite recipe of: Joe Ferrer, Jockey Agent, New Orleans, Louisiana

ZUCCHINI FRITTATA

"A frittata is a flat omelet with a medley of vegetables and herbs mixed into it. This recipe calls for zucchini and chard, but you can substitute any summer squash for the zucchini, and spinach for the chard."

2 tablespoons salad oil
1 small onion, finely chopped
1 clove garlic, pressed
2 large Swiss chard leaves, including stems, coarsely chopped
1 medium zucchini, coarsely chopped
6 eggs
⅛ teaspoon pepper
¼ teaspoon dry basil
¼ teaspoon oregano leaves
1 cup grated Parmesan cheese

Heat oil in a skillet over medium-high heat. Add onion, garlic, chard and zucchini; cook, stirring occasionally, until vegetables are soft, about 5 minutes. Remove from heat and let cool slightly. Beat eggs lightly with pepper, basil and oregano. Stir in cheese and vegetables. Pour into a greased 9-inch pie pan. Bake in a 350° oven for 25-30 minutes or until puffed and browned. Serve hot or at room temperature.
Serves: 6

Favorite recipe of: The Editor "Great for light lunch served with
fresh fruit salad or pasta salad."

ITALIAN TOMATO SAUCE

¼ cup olive oil
¾ cup chopped onion
2 cloves garlic, finely chopped
1 28-ounce can tomatoes
1 6½-ounce can tomato paste
1 6½-ounce can water
½ teaspoon oregano leaves
½ teaspoon basil leaves
1 teaspoon sugar
1 teaspoon salt
¼ teaspoon pepper

Heat oil in skillet. Add onion and garlic and cook over medium heat until tender. Add tomatoes which have been cut up fine and mashed, tomato paste, water, oregano, basil, sugar, salt and pepper. Cover and simmer 45 minutes. Serve over hot spaghetti.
Serves: 6

Favorite recipe of: Thomas S. Sweeney, Senior Vice President and General Manager of
Louisiana Downs, Bossier City, Louisiana

AMORGHU
(Garlic Sauce)

1 whole head garlic
1 teaspoon salt
⅓ cup olive oil
2 fresh overripe tomatoes, skinned, seeded and chopped
1 teaspoon oregano
2 tablespoons fresh parsley, chopped
½ teaspoon white pepper
Juice of 1 lemon
Yellow rind of ½ lemon, chopped

The secret to making this sauce is to first mash the garlic and salt together in a small wooden bowl with a mallet until it is pureed. DO NOT USE A BLENDER; garlic must be mashed. Mix remaining ingredients and add to garlic. Sauce may be used immediately, or covered and kept in the refrigerator for 1 week.
Use this delicious sauce over broiled lobster, fish or any seafood; over broiled steak, chicken or any plain cooked meat; or over salad. This sauce may be used to season meat or fish before cooking and used after as well.
Yield: 1½ cups

Original recipe of: Frances Zuppardo, New Orleans, Louisiana
Career Highlights: Frances describes herself as a racing enthusiast and breeder. She is the owner of *Zuppardo's Prince* currently standing at Clear Creek Stud in Folsom, Louisiana.

WOK SAUCE

"A simple little concoction to use with anything you might cook in a wok. I stir fry chicken or pork or shrimp pieces with ginger, onion and fresh broccoli or snow peas (even shredded cabbage). After all of these are tender, add:
1 tablespoon cornstarch
2 tablespoons Hoisom Sauce
¼ cup soy sauce
⅓ cup sherry
½ fresh lime, squeezed

Mix cornstarch, Hoisom sauce and soy sauce together before adding sherry and lime juice. Add to prepared food in wok. Heat and stir until slightly thickened and serve.

Favorite recipe of: Bill and Laurie Lussky, Louisville, Kentucky
Career Highlights: Bill has a farm outside of Louisville called Belmont Farm. Orange and blue racing colors were inherited from his grandfather, Cliff Lussky. Laurie was co-chairman of the Louisville Junior League "Cooking Book" and wrote a small historical cookbook in 1976 to benefit the Louisville historic houses, "Locust Grove" and "Farmington". Laurie is currently on the cookbook committee for the Kentucky Derby Museum publishing a cookbook and entertainment guide to be sold in the gift shop.

BACKSTRETCH BARBECUE SAUCE

Tom Ainslie claims that this sauce has pleased palates and penalized intestinal tracts on many a backstretch. "I have mixed it with Carolina-style chopped barbecue," he says. "I have brushed it onto back ribs while smoking them on green hickory," he goes on. "I have seen it bring tears to the eyes of Hardboots, who seldom cry. Every time a Boot named Brumfield sees me, he clutches at his abdomen."

For two pounds of back ribs or chopped barbecue, and a larger quantity of pork loin chops or grilled chicken, or whatever you like a highly seasoned sauce on. Note about smoke flavor. It should come from a wood or charcoal fire, not from a bottle. Users of bottled smoke are invited to leave without further delay.

Tom Ainslie

Scant ¼ cup light molasses
½ cup chopped onion
2-3 minced cloves of garlic
3 whole cloves
Juice of ½ orange
4 narrow strips orange rind, diced
Juice of 1 lemon
1 tablespoon cider vinegar
1 tablespoon dry mustard
½ teaspoon salt or to taste
Plenty of freshly ground black pepper
1 tablespoon steak sauce or Chinese oyster sauce
Tabasco, hot pepper flakes, or chopped fresh hot chili peppers to taste.
        Start slow. You can always add more.
8 ounces of ketchup

Put the liquids in a blender, then the solids. Pulse a few times until the garlic, onions and citrus peels have been chopped fine, but not until the sauce loses texture. Then pour into a pot and heat to the boil, stirring occasionally. If you have no blender, just chop the onions, garlic and citrus peels as fine as you can and go straight to the cookpot. The stuff can be used as a baste as grilled meats approach completion, and/or can be added with great success at the table.

Favorite recipe of: Tom Ainslie, Millwood, New York
Career Highlights: Tom Ainslie's books about the art of handicapping are the all-time
                    best sellers in that field. He also is a hard-knocking cook who
                    specializes in emphatic flavors. Otherwise, he lectures, goes racing
                    and maintains a low profile. As befits his standing as a grandfather,
                    he is over 21.

"Backstretch — Straight part of track on far side; stable area."

CANTEY'S CAROLINA BARBECUE SAUCE

2 cups tomato sauce
2 cups white vinegar
2 cups Worcestershire sauce
2 cups water
2 cups brown sugar
1 tablespoon chili powder, or to taste

Mix all ingredients in suitable pot and slowly boil until sauce becomes thick, about 45 minutes. Use brush to apply to spare ribs, chicken, pork chops, etc. while cooking on charcoal fire.
Yield: 2 quarts

Favorite recipe of: Joe Cantey, Trainer, Garden City, New York
Career Highlights: Trained such super stars as: *Cox's Ridge, Temperence Hill, Miss Baja, Lucy's Axe, Eminency, Dew Line, Majesty's Prince* and *Baby Kobe*

KENTUCKY BARBECUE SAUCE

1 teaspoon pepper
1 teaspoon brown sugar
1 teaspoon garlic salt
2 teaspoons salt
1 cup cider vinegar
1 5-ounce bottle Worcestershire sauce
4 tablespoons butter

Boil 2 cups water in saucepan with pepper. Simmer for 5 minutes, then add brown sugar, garlic salt, salt, vinegar and ½ bottle Worcestershire sauce. Simmer 5 minutes and add remaining Worcestershire sauce. Add butter and stir until melted. Marinate steaks in sauce several hours before barbecuing.
"It has always been my experience that most all 'horsey' people, owners, trainers, jockey's, etc., are steak eaters. Anywhere you see racetrack stickers on cars, you know the food is good, that's for sure! My husband was great at barbecuing steaks. His favorite was with Kentucky Barbecue Sauce. Could eat one right now!!" Mary Ann Combest
Yield: 1 quart

Origin: Nick Combest family in Columbia, Kentucky
Favorite recipe of: Mary Ann Combest, Franklin Square, New York
Racing interests: "Nick Combest, my husband, was a jockey at the New York and Florida tracks for 15 years, then became a trainer for 12 more years. Seven years ago, Nick died in an automobile accident."

"Hardboot — A Kentucky horseman of the old school, because of the legendary mud caked on his boots."

STEAK SAUCE FOR BARBECUE

½ cup butter
½ can (6 ounces) beer
¾ cup prepared barbecue sauce

Combine above ingredients in small saucepan. Brush sauce on steaks while on grill.
Yield: 1 pint

Favorite recipe of: Wendy Smith, Jockey Agent, Bossier City, Louisiana
Career Highlights: In 1982, working for Larry Snyder, Wendy remembers
Larry's record of 4500 career wins.

MEDIUM WHITE SAUCE

2 tablespoons butter
2 tablespoons flour
¼ teaspoon salt
⅛ teaspoon pepper
1 cup milk

Melt butter over low heat in a heavy saucepan. Using a wooden spoon for stirring, blend in flour and seasonings. Cook over low heat, stirring until mixture is smooth and bubbly. Remove from heat and stir in milk. Bring to a boil, stirring constantly and boil for 1 minute.
Variation: Cheese Sauce ½ cup Cheddar cheese, shredded
¼ teaspoon dry mustard
Stir into medium White Sauce while heating.
Yield: 1 cup

Origin: Tony "Bonesy" Cappola
Favorite recipe of: Darrel Haire, Jockey, Hot Springs, Arkansas

WHITE SAUCE THE EASY WAY

½ cup butter
3 tablespoons flour
2 pints light cream
Salt, pepper and cayenne to taste

Melt butter, add flour and stir. Add cream slowly and continue stirring until sauce thickens.
"This is a wonderful sauce with so many uses. It's great on angel hair spaghetti. Just add cheese and/or crabmeat. Be creative, and this sauce will help."
Yield: 1 quart

Original recipe of: Sandra Salmen, Publicity Director,
Fair Grounds Race Track, New Orleans, Louisiana

REMOULADE SAUCE-NEW ORLEANS STYLE

6 tablespoons olive oil
2 tablespoons white wine vinegar
1 tablespoon paprika
4 teaspoons Creole mustard, or stone ground (not Dijon creamy)
½ teaspoon freshly ground pepper
1 small onion, chopped fine
2-3 stalks celery, strings removed and chopped fine
1 tablespoon horseradish
Freshly chopped parsley, to taste
Salt, to taste

Puree ingredients in blender and salt to taste. Chill and serve over boiled shrimp. Should be "zingy" but not "red" hot.
Note: May be mixed by hand, but will separate. Stir well before serving.
Yield: 1½ cups

Favorite recipe of: Laurel Hauer, Placing Judge, Fair Grounds Race Track,
New Orleans, Louisiana

VINCENT T'S REMOULADE SAUCE

4 cups mayonnaise
1 cup dark Creole mustard
1 cup horseradish
1 cup finely chopped celery
1 cup finely chopped parsley
Garlic to taste, about 3 large pods, finely minced

Mix all ingredients and refrigerate for several hours to allow flavors to blend. Serve over shrimp or crawfish tails on a bed of lettuce.
Yield: 2 quarts

Original recipe of: Vincent Timphony, New Orleans, Louisiana
Career Highlights: Trainer of *Wild Again,* Black Chip Stable's winner of the Inaugural
Breeders' Cup Classic.

"Season — The period in which racing is conducted on a particular circuit or at a particular track; of a filly or mare, the period of estrus or 'heat'."

PLETCHER'S GARDEN SALSA

4 medium tomatoes, peeled, seeded and diced
6 green onions, chopped
1 can ripe, black olives, sliced
1 tablespoon garlic salt
2 fresh green chilies, chopped or 1 can chopped green chilies
1 tablespoon vinegar
1 tablespoon olive oil

Mix all ingredients together. Serve with corn chips. Can also be served by spreading softened cream cheese on a serving dish and topping with sauce. Also served with corn chips.
Yield: About 10 ounces

Favorite recipe of: J. J. Pletcher, Trainer, Benton, Louisiana
Career Highlights: Bill Shoemaker got his 500th career stakes win aboard
          Jeahene's Lark for Pletcher in the 1970 Sunny Slope Stakes.

FIG STRAWBERRY JAM

6 cups ripe figs, mashed
6 cups sugar
4 3-ounce packages Strawberry Jello

Combine mashed figs, sugar and Jello. Place over medium heat and stir constantly for 45-50 minutes. When cooked, seal in Mason pint jars. "During fig season, this recipe makes strawberry jam for cold winter biscuits."
Yield: 4 pints

Origin: Aunt Phine
Favorite recipe of: Janet P. Stemmans, the "Tack Lady", Stemmans, Inc.,
    Carencro, Louisiana

HOT PEPPER JELLY

1½ cups chopped bell pepper, seeds removed
4 pods hot pepper, seeds removed
1½ cups cider vinegar
6½ cups sugar
2 packages Certo
½ teaspoon salt
3 capfuls green food coloring

In a food processor or blender, chop the bell pepper and hot peppers with a little vinegar. In a pot combine the remaining vinegar, salt, peppers and sugar. Boil for 3 minutes. Add Certo and bring to a full boil for 1 minute. Remove from heat and stir in food coloring. Let stand for 5 minutes. Pour into 6 8-ounce sterilized jars and seal. Good on Ritz crackers spread with cream cheese.
Note: Wear rubber gloves to cut and clean hot peppers. Do not touch your face while preparing the peppers. Rinse the processor or blender with vinegar.
Yield: 6 jars

Favorite recipe of: Joan Pletcher, Benton, Louisiana
Career Highlights: Thoroughbred owner and wife of trainer, J. J. Pletcher.

Winner's Circle

Desserts

Cakes

Pies

Cookies

The following recipes were contributed by Laurie Lussky of Louisville, Kentucky. As co-chairman of the Louisville Junior League "Cooking Book" and author of a small historical cookbook in 1976, Laurie has earned quite a reputation as an excellent cook. In 1983, Laurie spent six weeks in Paris taking the advanced cooking course at LaVerenne and classes with Chef Ferre, the pastry chef at the famous Parisian restaurant, Maxim's. I am grateful to Laurie for these delicious delicacies.

CHEF FERRE'S MOKA CUPS

1½ pounds covering chocolate or 1 pound semi sweet chocolate,
    5 ounces butter and 4 tablespoons oil
250 small cordial beans
Ganache:
    5 ounces covering chocolate or semi sweet chocolate
    1 ounce cocoa butter, optional
    ⅔ cup heavy cream
    1 teaspoon instant coffee dissolved in 2 teaspoons hot water
1 box paper candy casing

Melt the chocolate over warm water (not in). Cover cookie sheet with foil. Separate paper cups into 3 or 4 together. Hold on to rim and dip cut into chocolate all around. Place bottom down on foil. Leave to set. (Will coat 60 cups.)
For Ganache: Melt chocolate (and cocoa butter) over warm water. Bring cream to a boil and add to chocolate. Mix well. Add dissolved coffee and mix well again.
Remove cups from chocolate carefully. Place 2 candy coffee beans in each chocolate cup. Fill pastry bag with ganache and pipe a rosette into each cup. Top each with a candy coffee bean.
Yield: Approximately 60 Moka Cups

Origin: Chef Ferre, Pastry Chef at Maxim's Restaurant, Paris, France

CHOCOLATE MACAROONS

1 cup almond paste
3 eggs
2¾ cups powdered sugar
¼ cup cocoa
¼ teaspoon almond extract

Mix these ingredients together well. Line a cookie sheet with parchment or brown paper. Drop dough from a teaspoon onto paper. Bake at 350° for 15 to 20 minutes. Let cool, then pour a little water under paper to aid in removing macaroons.
Yield: 2 dozen macaroons

Favorite recipe of: Laurie Lussky, Louisville, Kentucky

ORANGINES
"Orange Marzipan Candies"

5 ounces candied orange peel, very finely chopped
2 tablespoons Grand Marnier
1 pound marzipan
Powdered sugar for rolling
1 pound covering chocolate or ¾ pound semi-sweet chocolate,
    ¼ pound butter, and 3 tablespoons oil

*Combine the chopped orange peel and Grand Marnier until well blended.
Roll into a ball and coat with powdered sugar. Cover and chill 30 minutes.
Cover 2 baking sheets with foil. Sprinkle work surface with powdered sugar. Roll out the almond mixture ⅜ inches thick. Stamp out rounds with ¾ or
1-inch cookie cutter. Place rounds on cookie sheets to dry over night.
The next day, melt the covering chocolate or semi sweet chocolate, butter
and oil. Dip eacn candy into barely warm chocolate, wipe off excess and
place on foil lined baking sheet.
Garnish with a diamond shaped cut of candied orange peel.*

Origin: Chef Ferre, Pastry Chef at Maxim's Restaurant, Paris, France

CARAMEL APPLES

4 cups sugar
Pinch salt
¾-1 cup milk
½ cup unsalted butter
1 teaspoon vanilla
Apples on sticks

*Caramelize 1 cup sugar in heavy, small skillet. In another pan place 3 cups
sugar, salt, and milk. Stir constantly until sugar dissolves and it comes to a
boil. Wipe sides of pan clear of sugar crystals and place a lid on for 1 minute
to help clear sides (otherwise it will become grainy later on). Cook slowly
now, add caramelized sugar and boil to 238°. Pour into bowl. Add butter and
let cool about 20 minutes. Add vanilla and beat until creamy. Dip in apples
on sticks.*
Yield: 10-12

Origin: Laurie Lussky's mother's recipe. Laurie writes, "Every Halloween
       we make about a hundred of these for treats. Mother used to make
       50 in Atlanta and drive to Louisville with them to help me! Of course you can
       also use this as icing on jam cake or drop by spoonfuls for pralines."

CONFIRMATION PASTRIES

1 pound sharp cheese, shredded
1½ cups unsalted butter
3 cups flour
Cinnamon
Pecans, 90-100 halves
Dates, 2 8-ounce packages
Powdered sugar

Mix cheese and butter. Add flour and chill. Roll thin. Cut with biscuit cutter and wrap around a date stuffed with a pecan half. Sprinkle with cinnamon and seal ends. Bake in a 375° oven for 20 minutes. Roll in powdered sugar while hot.
Yield: Approximately 90-100 pastries

Favorite recipe of: Laurie Lussky, Member of the Cookbook Committee,
Kentucky Derby Museum, Louisville, Kentucky

JUDY'S DIAMOND CUPS

18 squares semisweet chocolate
3 tablespoons vegetable shortening
1 large can crushed pineapple
1 4-ounce box pistachio instant pudding
1 9-ounce container frozen whipped topping
1 cup cherries, drained, chopped
1 cup pecans, chopped
1 tablespoon lemon juice
8 stemmed cherries

Chocolate Cups: Melt chocolate and shortening in top of double boiler over hot water. Remove from heat. Spread thin layer of chocolate over inside of 8 large pleated foil cup cake liners. If sides of cups are thin, place in muffin pan cups. Refrigerate 1 hour or until firm. Coat a second time. (Extra chocolate can be used for dipping stemmed cherries for topping.)
Filling: Mix pineapple and juice with pudding mix. Fold in whipped topping, cherries, pecans, and lemon juice. Mix well. Fill chocolate cups and top with chocolate dipped cherries. Will keep well in refrigerator for 1 week.
Serves: 8

Original recipe of: Judy A. Behler, New Orleans, Louisiana
Career Highlights: Owner and breeder of the race mare, *Judy's Diamond,* who won four of her first five starts and as of 1984 has collected over $125,000 in winnings. Judy writes, "My biggest thrill was when *Judy's Diamond* defeated Horse of the Year, *Monique Rene,* at the Fair Grounds.

TURTLES
"Our Fastest Horse"

1 pound caramels
2 tablespoons evaporated milk
1 tablespoon butter
2-2½ cups broken pecans
1 pound Hershey bars
½ large sheet parafin

Place caramels, milk and butter in 1 quart measuring cup. Heat in microwave on roast for 4 or 5 minutes or until melted. Mix broken pecans in caramel mixture. Using a teaspoon, form turtles and place on waxed paper or plastic wrap. Refrigerate uncovered for 30 minutes. Place chocolate and parafin in a double boiler. When melted, remove caramel candies from refrigerator and drop 2 or 3 at a time in chocolate. Place chocolate covered turtles on waxed paper or plastic wrap. Keep chocolate on low heat until all candy has been dipped. Refrigerate turtles 20-30 minutes before serving.
Yield: Approximately 3 dozen

Origin: Joy Boudreaux

Favorite recipe of: Janet P. Stemmans, "Tack Lady", Stemmans, Inc. Carencro, Louisiana

CHOCOLATE COVERED TURTLES

1 12-ounce package milk chocolate chips
2 tablespoons oil
1 14-ounce package caramels
¼ cup butter
⅛ cup light cream
1 cup coarsely chopped pecans

Melt chocolate chips and oil together in a double boiler. Pour half of the melted chocolate into a 9-inch buttered square pan. Let cool. Melt together caramels, butter and cream. Add pecans and pour over cooled chocolate in pan. Again, allow to cool. Spread remaining chocolate on top. Cool and cut into small bite-sized squares.
Yield: Approximately 3 dozen

Favorite recipe of: Patrick J. Pope, Racing Secretary
Louisiana Downs, Bossier City, Louisiana

"Racing secretary— Official who prescribes conditions of races at his track and usually serves as track handicapper, assigning weights to entrants in handicap races."

FUDGE

3 cups sugar
¾ cup butter
⅔ cup evaporated milk
1 12-ounce package chocolate chips
1 7-ounce jar marshmallow cream
1 teaspoon vanilla
1 cup chopped nuts, optional

Mix sugar, butter and evaporated milk in heavy saucepan. Boil for 5 minutes then remove from stove. Add chocolate chips, marshmallow cream and vanilla. Stir mixture quickly until creamy. Add nuts and turn into 9x13-inch greased pan. Cool for 1½ hours and cut into pieces.
Yield: 2 dozen

Origin: Mrs. Larry (Jeanette) Snyder
Favorite recipe of: Larry Snyder, Jockey, Hot Springs, Arkansas
Career Highlights: Hall of Fame rider who has won over 5,000 races; swept the
                    Ohio, Hawthorne and American Derbies aboard *Silver Series*
                    in 1977; won the 1980 Sorority Stakes aboard *Fancy Naskra;* won
                    the 1983 Count Fleet Handicap aboard *Dave's Friend;* won the
                    1970 Oaklawn Handicap with *Charlie Jr.*

WINNERS' TREAT

½ cup butter or margarine
1 box powdered sugar
1 cup crunchy peanut butter
4 cups Rice Krispies
1 8-ounce Hershey bar
6 ounces semi-sweet chocolate bits
1 bar parafin

Melt butter in large saucepan. Stir in powdered sugar and peanut butter. Mix until well blended and fold in Rice Krispies. Form into 2-inch balls and chill in refrigerator for 1 hour. In a double boiler, melt Hershey bar, chocolate bits and parafin. Dip balls in chocolate mixture and put on waxed paper to harden. When chocolate is firm, wrap each ball in plastic wrap and store in refrigerator.
Serves: 12-15

Favorite recipe of: Howard L. Battle, Racing Secretary, Keeneland
                    Race Course, Lexington, Kentucky

"Handicap — Race in which racing secretary or track handicapper assigns weights designed to equalize winning chances of entrants; to study horses' records in effort to determine winner of race."

HEAVENLY HASH

12-ounce package chocolate chips
1 14-ounce can sweetened condensed milk
1 cup coarsely chopped pecans
1 10-ounce bag marshmallows

In a double boiler or large non-stick saucepan, melt chips, stir in milk, then remove from heat. Add pecans and marshmallows and stir gently to coat with chocolate. Spread evenly into greased 9 x 13-inch pan and refrigerate. Cut into squares. Easy and quick to make. Good dessert to carry to suppers.
Serves: 24

Origin: Ruby Hopkins
Favorite recipe of: Charlotte Stemmans, daughter of Don and Janet Stemmans.
　　　　　　　　Charlotte works in the Stemmans' Tack Shop,
　　　　　　　　Carencro, Louisiana

TOFFEE

1 cup butter
1 cup white sugar
2 cups finely chopped pecans
½ cup semi sweet chocolate chips
½ cup milk chocolate chips

In a cast iron skillet or a Dutch oven, melt butter. Stir in sugar gradually. Stirring constantly with a wooden spoon, bring to a bubble. Make sure butter and sugar do not separate and that mixture remains bubbly. Bring mixture to 290° on a candy thermometer. Once mixture reaches 290° remove from heat. Add 1 cup chopped pecans. Place on a jelly roll pan, patting down with a rubber spatula to ¼-⅓-inch thickness. Sprinkle with chocolate chips and swirl with spatula, do not spread.
Sprinkle remaining pecans on top and press with back of spatula. Cool for 20 minutes. Put into refrigerator for 2 hours. When ready to serve, break into pieces.
Serves: 10-12

Origin: Mrs. Patrick (Jeanne) Pope
Favorite recipe of: Patrick J. Pope, Racing Secretary, Louisiana Downs,
　　　　　　　　Bossier City, Louisiana

APRICOT SQUARES

2 cups sifted flour
1 cup sugar
¼ teaspoon cream of tartar
½ pound butter or margarine
5 egg yolks
1 18-ounce jar apricot preserves

Sift flour, sugar and cream of tartar together. Cut in the butter or margarine as for a pie crust. Add egg yolks and mix well. With your hands, pat about ¾ of the dough into a 15½ x 10½-inch cookie sheet as evenly as possible with sides a little higher than center portion. Spread dough with the preserves. Roll remaining dough on a well-floured board, adding a little flour if the dough is hard to handle. Cut dough into strips and arrange in lattice fashion over preserves. Bake at 375° until nicely browned, about 30-35 minutes. Cool before cutting into squares.
Yield: About 70 squares

Favorite recipe of: Cloyce K. Box, Thoroughbred Owner, Frisco, Texas

JOHN HENRY BARS

"They're a winner every time, no matter how many times you run them!"

⅔ cup margarine
4 cups oatmeal (not oats, horse fans!)
1 cup brown sugar
2 teaspoons vanilla
½ cup corn syrup
Topping:
1 cup chocolate chips
⅔ cup peanut butter

Melt margarine and add rest of ingredients. Spread into WELL GREASED 9x13-inch pan. Bake at 350° until bubbly, about 25-30 minutes. Cool. Melt topping ingredients and blend thoroughly. Spread on top of cooled oatmeal mixture in pan. Put in refrigerator to set, about 1 hour. Cut into bars.
Yield: 12 large bars

Favorite recipe of: David E. Hager, II, Paris, Kentucky
Career Highlights: Manager of Idle Hour Farm for Mrs. Julian G. Rogers, David Hager's aunt.

"John Henry — 1984 Horse of the Year and racing's first $6 million earner."

BURNED CRISP
(Apple Crisp)

6 medium tart apples, sliced
2 tablespoons lemon juice
1 teaspoon cinnamon
¼ teaspoon cloves
¼ cup brown sugar
1 cup raisins
2 tablespoons flour
¼ cup apple juice
Nuts, coconut to taste
Topping:
2 cups quick cooking oats
½ cup brown sugar
*¼ cup wheat germ
⅓ cup flour
1 teaspoon cinnamon
½ cup butter
*Substitution: ⅔ cup flour may be used instead of the wheat germ.

Toss together apples, lemon juice, spices, sugar, raisins, flour, nuts and coconut. Spread in lightly greased 8x12-inch baking pan and sprinkle with apple juice. For topping, mix together oats, wheat germ, flour, sugar and cinnamon. Cut in butter to make crumbly mixture. Press topping lightly over apples and bake in a 350° oven for about 30 minutes or until apples are tender and topping is browned and crisp. Serve with whipped cream or ice cream.
Serves: 6

Origin: Old family recipe
Favorite recipe of: Mr. and Mrs. Roger Bronzine
Career Highlights: Owners of Ionian Farm in Ocala, Florida. The title of this recipe
                    is named after their broodmare *Burned Crisp.*

BAKED PINEAPPLE

¼ pound butter
2 eggs, beaten
4 slices cubed bread
½ cup sugar
1 20-ounce can crushed pineapple, well-drained
1 handful miniature marshmallows
1 small can evaporated milk, ⅔ cup

Melt butter and mix together with eggs, bread, sugar and pineapple. Fold in marshmallows. Put in greased 8 x 8-inch baking dish. Pour evaporated milk over this and bake at 350° for 30 minutes. ENJOY!
Serves: 4 "This recipe is so good, you'd do well to double it."

Origin: Atlanta, Georgia
Favorite recipe of: Rod Seiling, Ontario, Canada
Career Highlights: NFL Hockey Player for 15 years; former racetrack manager;
presently the Executive Vice President of Racetracks of
Canada, Inc.

LUCILLE'S EASY BLACKBERRY COBBLER

½ cup butter or margarine
1 cup flour
1 cup sugar
1 cup milk
1½ teaspoon baking powder
1 16-ounce can blackberries
⅔ cup sugar

Melt butter or margarine in 2-quart casserole. Mix flour, sugar, milk and baking powder and beat well. Pour batter over melted butter. Heat blackberries and ⅔ cup sugar in saucepan until well blended. Pour over batter. Bake at 350° for 30 minutes or until brown. Good served warm. warm.
Serves: 4-6

Favorite recipe of: Woody Stephens, Trainer, Long Island, New York
Career Highlights: In 1984, Woody Stephens was the top stakes-winning
trainer for the second year in a row, winning 36 added-
money events with 109 starters, a .330 batting average.
He was also tops in stakes earnings.

WINNER'S CIRCLE BROWNIES

2 cups self-rising flour
1 teaspoon vanilla extract
1 teaspoon almond extract
2 cups sugar
1⅓ cups Wesson oil
½ cup cocoa
4 eggs, slightly beaten
1 cup chopped pecans
Icing:
1 cup sugar
¼ cup cocoa
¼ cup margarine
¼ cup milk
½ teaspoon vanilla extract
1 teaspoon almond extract

Combine all ingredients for brownies and mix by hand. Pour into 11 x 14-inch pan. Bake 30 minutes in 350° oven. Cool. Combine all ingredients for Icing in saucepan. Bring to a full boil. Cook 1 minute. Remove from heat and set in a pan of cold water. Spread on cooled brownies when it begins to thicken.
Yield: 4-5 dozen

Origin: Mrs. Cot (Anne Dodd) Campbell
Favorite recipe of: W. Cothran Campbell, President, Dogwood Farm, Inc.
Greenville, Georgia
Career Highlights: Cot Campbell's Dogwood Farm is a Georgia-based 422 acre training facility for thoroughbred racehorses with offices in Atlanta. Prior to his career in the racing industry, Campbell was board chairman of Burton-Campbell, Inc., one of the South's largest advertising agencies. Campbell is a trustee for the Thoroughbred Owners and Breeders Association of America. He is also a member of the Thoroughbred Club of America, Lexington, and The Turf Club of London. In Georgia, he is a member of the Piedmont Driving Club, Atlanta Rotary Club and The Peachtree Presbyterian Church. He is a trustee of the Georgia Horse Foundation and one of the founders of the Atlanta Hunt and Steeplechase.

"Turn out — To send a horse to the farm for pasturage and rest."

BREAD PUDDING A LA BUNNY

2 cups milk
2 cups soft bread crumbs
3 eggs, separated
¾ cup sugar
1 teaspoon vanilla
½ cup raisins, optional
1 tablespoon butter
6 tablespoons sugar

Pour 1 cup milk over bread and let soak in baking dish. Beat egg yolks until light and add sugar, vanilla and remaining 1 cup milk. Pour this over soaked bread crumbs. If using raisins, sprinkle over mixture. Cut butter into small pieces and distribute evenly over top. Bake about 30 minutes at 350°. Beat egg whites until very stiff, adding sugar gradually. Spread over pudding and brown. This is wonderful served with a creme sauce.
Serves: 8

Origin: Mrs. J. E. (Bunny) Jumonville, Jr.'s great grandmother, Tillie Wilbert
Favorite recipe of: Senator J. E. Jumonville, Jr., Ventress, Louisiana
Career Highlights: Thoroughbred Owner, Farmer, Rancher and State Senator

JOHN'S CINNAMON BREAD PUDDING

1 16-ounce loaf cinnamon raisin bread
1 quart milk
3 eggs
2 cups sugar
2 tablespoons vanilla extract
1 tablespoon butter

Preheat oven to 350°. Tear bread into 2-inch pieces, drop in a large mixing bowl and pour milk over. Toss until coated and let bread soak 15 minutes. Beat eggs with sugar until light yellow, smooth and thick. Add vanilla. Pour over bread and mix until bread is coated with egg mixture. Transfer to a buttered 9x13x2-inch baking dish and place dish (uncovered) in another pan containing 1-2 inches of water. Place dishes in oven and bake until set, when knife inserted into center comes out clean, about 1 hour. Serve with heavy cream or whipped cream. Best served warm.
Serves: 10

Favorite recipe of: John Oxley, Trainer, Shreveport, Louisiana
Career Highlights: Trainer of *A Letter To Harry*, winner of 22 races, 13 stake
races and over $600,000.00, undefeated in three seasons
of racing at the Fair Grounds in New Orleans. Trained
Turbulence, winner of six stakes at Louisiana Downs and
$300,000.00, won the Phoenix Handicap at Keeneland,
the oldest stake race in the country. Trained *Lady Vi-E*
winner of the Kentucky Oaks.

"Oaks — Stakes race for three-year-old fillies."

DAILY DOUBLE DELIGHT

1st layer:
½ cup margarine
1 cup flour
2 tablespoons sugar
½ cup pecans, chopped fine
2nd layer:
1 package cream cheese, softened
1 cup whipped topping
1 cup powdered sugar
3rd layer:
4 egg yolks
3 cups milk
2 cups sugar
5 tablespoons flour
2 tablespoons cocoa
1 tablespoon vanilla
4th layer:
9-ounce container whipped topping

1st layer: Mix together and press evenly into bottom of 9x12-inch pan. Bake at 350° for 15 minutes. Let cool.
2nd layer: Mix ingredients and spread on top of first layer.
3rd layer: Mix together all ingredients except vanilla. Cook over medium heat stirring constantly. When thick, add vanilla and beat. Pour onto 2nd layer. Refrigerate until cool.
4th layer: Top with whipped topping. Cut into squares to serve.
Serves: 12

Favorite recipe of: Julio Espinoza, Jockey, Louisville, Kentucky
Career Highlights: Riding in the Kentucky Derby five times, hoping someday to win it.

"Daily Double — Form of mutuel betting in which player attempts to pick winners of two races, buying a single ticket on the double choice."

ROYAL PRUNER'S NOODLE PUDDIN

8-ounce package wide egg noodles
2 eggs, beaten
1 cup sugar
2 teaspoons cinnamon
2 tablespoons vanilla
1 cup raisins
1 pint ricotta cheese
½ cup butter or margarine
1 16-ounce can crushed pineapple
1 small jar cherries, drained, chopped
1 can cherry pie filling

Boil noodles for 9 minutes; drain and rinse well. Set aside. In a large bowl, mix eggs, vanilla, cinnamon, butter and cheese for 1 minute. Add raisins, pineapple and cherries. Mixture will be thin. Add noodles and mix for about 30 seconds. Pour mixture into a 9x13x2-inch baking dish, ungreased. Bake at 325° for 1 hour. Remove and add the pie filling to cover top, set about 1 inch from the sides. Bake for additional 30 minutes at 300°. Allow to cool a little before cutting into squares and serving. For best results, cut into 3 inch squares and serve using a spatula.
Serves: 8

Favorite recipe of: Michelle Glusman, Plantation, Florida
Career Highlights: Thoroughbred owner and racing enthusiast, Michelle writes, "Cooking is fun, but horse racing is great. I first enjoyed this dish after the maiden win of *Royal Pruner* beating *Island Whirl.* I hope you'll make it and feel like a winner too!" *Royal Pruner* is still owned by the GLussman's and is standing at stud at Southland Farm in Ocala, Florida.

TREE LINE FARM PERSIMMON PUDDING

1 egg
1 cup persimmon pulp
2 cups sugar
2 cups flour
1 teaspoon soda
1 quart whole milk

Mix all ingredients together on low speed with mixer. Pour into buttered pan or casserole. Bake at 250° for 2-3 hours, stirring occasionally. Color will be dark brown. May be served with vanilla ice cream while still warm, or cold with whipped cream.
Serves: 8-10

Origin: Old family favorite enjoyed through the holidays and has become a Tree Line Farm tradition
Favorite recipe of: Mr. and Mrs. Blanton W. Cooper, Tree Line Farm, Elm Grove, Louisiana

CARAMEL RICE

1 teacup rice, uncooked
1 pint milk
1 vanilla pod or a large piece of lemon peel
4 ounces cream
6 ounces sugar
Juice of a lemon or orange
2 ounces candied citrus peel, finely chopped

Pour milk into top part of double boiler. Add rice, 4 tablespoons sugar and vanilla pod or lemon peel. Cover and let simmer until rice is cooked, about 1½-2 hours. Turn rice into a souffle dish and add lemon or orange juice and cream, which should be fairly thick. Add candied peel. Chill this mixture thoroughly. Heat broiler. Spread a layer of sugar on top of rice. Have the broiler already hot and place dish under it, fairly close to heat. In about 2 minutes, the surface will have turned to toffee on top. Remove from heat the second the sugar looks set, as it burns in no time. Refrigerate again. Serve very cold.
Serves: 4-6

Favorite recipe of: Alec Head, Trainer and Breeder, Hagyard Farm,
Lexington, Kentucky, Chantilly, France

JEWISH RICE CUSTARD

1 pound raw whole grain rice
pinch salt
6 quarts milk
12 large eggs
2 pounds sugar
Vanilla and almond flavoring, to taste
Cinnamon and nutmeg, to taste

Cook together on top of stove: rice, salt and milk. Cook until rice is just tender, stirring constantly to keep from sticking. Beat eggs with sugar until sugar is dissolved. When rice is tender, add egg-sugar mixture and continue cooking until mixture thickens. Pour into a large flat pan and stir in vanilla and almond flavoring as desired. Stir several times while cooling to keep the rice from settling to the bottom. When thoroughly cool, sprinkle with cinnamon and nutmeg to taste and store in refrigerator for several hours or overnight. It will thicken as it sets in the refrigerator. This custard will stay creamy and will not get dry like oven-baked custard.
**Serves: 30-40 Recipe can be reduced by one-half or one-fourth for
home use.**

Origin: Charles O. Long used to be an Offshore Steward. His recipe for Jewish Rice
Custard is one of the favorites enjoyed by the boys on the rig.
Favorite recipe of: Charles O. Long, Former Thoroughbred Owner,
New Orleans, Louisiana

COEUR A LA CREME FRAICHE

"This is a beautiful heart-shaped dessert that takes time to prepare, but is wonderful for a very special occasion. Betty Moran served it at a celebration dinner after *Creme Fraiche* won the Belmont."

Two days before serving, prepare Creme Fraiche:
1 pint heavy cream
½ pint sour cream

Blend creams over low heat to remove chill. Place in glass jar and leave at room temperature 8-10 hours; then refrigerate for at least 4 hours.

One day before serving, prepare mold:
¾ pound cottage cheese
8 ounces cream cheese
½ cup creme fraiche
1 tablespoon powdered sugar
½ cup heavy cream
3-cup heart-shaped, perforated mold
Cheese cloth

Mix cottage cheese, cream cheese and creme fraiche. Beat until smooth and add powdered sugar. In separate bowl whip heavy cream; fold into cheese mixture. Line bottom of mold with cheese cloth. Spoon mixture into mold and fold overlapping cloth over top. Place mold on a tray and refrigerate overnight. (Liquid whey will be released from mold as cheese mixture becomes firm.)

Several hours before serving, prepare Topping:
½ quart fresh strawberries or 2 10-ounce packages frozen strawberries
Fresh whole strawberries for garnish
1 cup sugar or ½ cup if using frozen strawberries
2 tablespoons kirsch liqueur

Mash berries and cook over low heat with sugar until soft then press through fine strainer. Add kirsch and chill.
To serve dessert:
Unfold cheese cloth and invert heart-shaped mold onto a serving plate. Pour sauce around dessert. Garnish with whole strawberries. Serve extra sauce on the side.
Serves: 5

Origin: Nancy Fasulo, Saratoga Springs, New York
Favorite recipe of: Mrs. Elizabeth Moran, Paoli, Pennsylvania
Career Highlights: Owner of *Creme Fraiche,* 1985 winner of the Belmont Stakes;
other graded stakes won include the 1984 What A Pleasure Stake,
and in 1985, the Kentucky Derby Trail, the American Derby
and the Jerome Derby.

FLAN

1 cup sugar
1 8-ounce package cream cheese
2 14-ounce cans condensed milk
1 13-ounce can evaporated milk
1 cup milk
6 eggs, beaten
1 teaspoon vanilla or grated rind of 1 lime

To caramelize sugar, melt over low heat. Pour melted sugar into a 2-quart pyrex mold or baking dish. Mix softened cream cheese until smooth and creamy. Gradually add condensed milk and continue stirring until well blended. Add remaining evaporated milk, whole milk and beaten eggs. Stir in vanila or grated lime rind. Pour into dish with caramel. Place dish into a larger pan with about 1-2 inches water. Bake in 350° oven for 1 hour. Make sure there is always water in the pan while flan is baking. Cool and chill in refrigerator for several hours. When ready to serve, use a knife to go around edge of dish and turn flan over onto a shallow dish.

Serves: 8 "Only 6,000 calories per serving!!!"

Origin: Mrs. Raul (Iris) Viera, New Orleans, Louisiana
Favorite recipe of: Joe Ferrer, Jockey Agent, New Orleans, Louisiana

ORANGE JUICE SOUP

Fresh squeezed orange juice
Fresh pineapple, cut in cubes
Green, seedless grapes
Navel oranges, diced
Fresh rasberries
Bananas, sliced
Optional: Fruits of the season may be substituted to your taste.

Squeeze 3 oranges per person. Add pineapple cubes, grapes, navel oranges, rasberries and top with bananas. DO NOT ADD WATER, DO NOT ADD SUGAR. Scoop into champagne glasses or dessert cups and put in freezer until slushy. Serve with meal or as a dessert with pound cake. May be kept in the freezer for several days and allowed to semi-thaw for 45 minutes when desired.
"Beautiful, delicious and a unique dish that causes much favorable comment when served."

Original recipe of: 'Gene Liss, Owner, The Missouri Stud, St. Louis, Missouri
Racing interests: Reasons for entering racing and breeding are "fun, profit and tax advantages for myself and my customers"; 'Gene Liss is Missouri's only registered bloodstock agent.

JOHN ED'S FAVORITE CHEESECAKE

1 cup (9 slices) zweiback crumbs
2 tablespoons sugar
2 tablespoons melted butter
½ cup sugar
2 8-ounce packages cream cheese, softened
1 teaspoon vanilla
¼ teaspoon salt
½ teaspoon grated lemon peel
2 cups sour cream
5 eggs, separated
1 tablespoon lemon juice
½ cup sugar

Crust: Mix crumbs, 2 tablespoon sugar and butter. Press into ungreased 9-inch springform pan.
Filling: Gradually beat ½ cup sugar into softened cream cheese. Beat in vanilla, salt and lemon peel. Add sour cream and blend in egg yolks. Beat egg whites with lemon juice to soft peaks, gradually adding ½ cup sugar, beating stiff, but not dry. Fold cheese mixture into egg whites. Pour into crumb crust and bake at 325° for 1¼ hours. Run knife around edge after removing from oven and cooling on wire rack for 10 minutes. Cool 1 hour before removing sides of pan. Chill. Serve with fresh fruit sauce or plain. Rich, but good!
Serves: 12

Favorite recipe of: John Ed Anthony, Thoroughbred Owner, Fordyce, Arkansas
Career Highlights: Owner of outstanding Thoroughbreds, *Cox's Ridge* and
            Temperence Hill.

BEST EVER CHEESE CAKE

1½ cups graham cracker crumbs
¼ cup sugar
⅓ cup melted butter
3 8-ounce packages cream cheese, softened
1 cup sugar
2 teaspoons vanilla
3 eggs, room temperature
1 cup sour cream

Blend crumbs, sugar and butter well and press an 8 or 9-inch spring form pan. Cream softened cream cheese and 1 cup sugar. Add eggs, 1 at a time. Blend in vanilla and sour cream. Bake in a 350° oven for 60-70 minutes. Turn oven off and open oven door slightly. Leave cheese cake in oven for an additional hour. Remove from oven and let cool. Refrigerate at least 4-6 hours.
Serves: 8-10

Origin: Mrs. Pat (Jeanne) Pope
Favorite recipe of: Patrick J. Pope, Racing Secretary,
            Louisiana Downs, Bossier City, Louisiana

CHOCOLATE CHIP CHEESECAKE

1½ cups finely crushed Oreo cookies, 18 cookies
¼ cup butter, melted
3 8-ounce packages cream cheese, softened
1 14-ounce can condensed milk
3 eggs
2 teaspoons vanilla extract
1 cup mini chocolate chips
1 teaspoon flour

Preheat oven to 300°. Combine crumbs and butter. Pat on bottom of 9-inch springform pan. In large mixing bowl, beat cheese until fluffy. Add condensed milk and beat until smooth. Add eggs and vanilla; mix well. In a small bowl, toss together ½ cup chocolate chips with flour to coat. Stir into cheese mixture. Pour into prepared pan. Sprinkle remaining chips over top. Bake for 1 hour or until cake springs back when lightly touched. Cool at room temperature. Chill for several hours before serving.
Serves: 8-10

Origin: Mrs. Gerald (Mona) Romero
Favorite recipe of: Gerald Romero, Trainer, Haughton, Louisiana
Career Highlights: Set an all time record breaking win percentage at
                    Louisiana Downs for 1984 with 30.3%; at age 28,
                    the youngest trainer to do so.

EASY FINISH CAKE

3 cups flour
2 cups sugar
1 teaspoon soda
1 teaspoon salt
1 teaspoon cinnamon
18-ounce can crushed pineapple, do not drain
1½ cups cooking oil
3 eggs, beaten
1½ teaspoons vanilla
1 cup chopped nuts
2 cups very ripe bananas, diced

Mix together, do not beat. Bake in greased and floured tube pan for approximately 1 hour and 20 minutes at 350°. Test after 1 hour with toothpick. "This is truly, 'Cake That Won't Last'."
Serves: 12

Origin: Mrs. Tony (Nancy) Foyt
Favorite recipe of: Tony Foyt, Trainer, Louisville, Kentucky

BOURBON COUNTY BEER CAKE

2 cups dark brown sugar, firmly packed
2 teaspoons baking soda
2 eggs
1 cup shortening
1½ cups chopped pecans
2 cups beer
3 cups flour
1 teaspoon cinnamon
1 teaspoon salt
1 teaspoon ground cloves
1 teaspoon allspice
Sauce:
½ cup margarine
1 cup sugar
3 egg yolks
½ cup boiling water
6 tablespoons whiskey
Whipped cream

In food processor, using steel blade, mix soda and brown sugar. Add the shortening and cream together. Add eggs and blend until smooth. Mix dry ingredients and add alternately with beer (too much liquid at one time may cause processor to leak). Add nuts. Pour into well-greased 10-inch tube pan and bake at 300° for 1½ hours, or until tests done with a toothpick. To make sauce, in saucepan, cream sugar and margarine; blend in egg yolks. Carefully blend in water; blend. Add whiskey and blend. Serve over beer cake with whipped cream.
Serves: 8-10

Favorite recipe of: David E. Hager, II, Manager, Idle Hour Farm, Paris, Kentucky

"Bourbon County (Paris, Kentucky) is truly in the heart of the Bluegrass. About 20 minutes northeast of Lexington, Paris is the home of many well known Thoroughbred farms; such as Circle "O", Claiborne, Forest View, Idle Hour, Katalpa, Stone, and Stonereath, to name only a few. It is in this small town and its surrounding area that such noted horses such as *Nijinsky II, Secretariat, Devil's Bag, Sir Ivor, Mr. Prospector, Northern Baby*, etc. have their homes."

MOTHER'S BANANA CAKE

3 cups sifted cake flour
2 teaspoons soda
1 cup shortening
2 cups sugar
¾ cup buttermilk
2 eggs, slightly beaten
1-1½ cups mashed ripe bananas, 3-4 medium
Frosting:
8-ounce package cream cheese, softened
½ cup butter, softened
1 box powdered sugar
2 teaspoons vanilla
1 cup chopped nuts

Line bottom of three 9-inch cake pans with waxed, greased paper. Sift together, flour and soda. Cream shortening thoroughly. Add sugar gradually and cream until light and fluffy. Add 2 tablespoons buttermilk, then eggs. Add dry ingredients and remaining buttermilk alternately beating thoroughly after each addition. Fold mashed bananas into batter and pour into cake pans. Bake in moderate 350° oven for 25-30 minutes. Test for doneness with toothpick. Cool on wire rack, remove layers and frost. Frosting: Cream cheese and butter. Add sugar and beat until smooth. Fold in nuts and vanilla. This cake is better the day after it is baked.
Serves: 12

Origin: Mrs. John (Alta) Franks
Favorite recipe of: John Franks, Shreveport, Louisiana
Career Highlights: Honored for two consecutive years (1983, 1984) as racing's
                    outstanding owner.

FINISH LINE SPONGE CAKE

6 eggs, separated
1½ cups sugar
1½ cups flour
2½ tablespoons cornstarch
2½ teaspoons baking powder
⅓ cup cold water
1 pint whipping cream
3 tablespoons sugar
2 egg whites
Fresh strawberries or blueberries

Beat egg yolks with half of the sugar (¾ cup) until creamy. Add flour, cornstarch, baking powder and water. In separate bowl, beat egg whites adding the rest of the sugar gradually until whites are stiff. Fold two mixtures together. Pour into two 9-inch round cake pans. Bake in preheated 350° oven for 30-35 minutes. For topping, beat egg whites until stiff. Beat whipping cream with 3 tablespoons sugar. Fold together. Serve cakes with whipped cream topping and fresh strawberries or blueberries on top and between layers.
Serves: 10

Favorite recipe of: John Oxley, Trainer, Shreveport, Louisiana
Career Highlights: A former New York steeplechase rider, Oxley has been training for more than three decades. Trained *A Letter to Harry,* one of the Midwest's most feared handicap horses in the late 1970's and *Lady Vi-E,* who won the Kentucky Oaks in 1970.

TRIFECTA FIG CAKE

2 cups sugar
2 eggs
½ cup margarine
1 cup whole milk
1 teaspoon cinnamon
2 teaspoon baking soda
1 teaspoon ginger
2 cups chopped fig preserves
2½ cups all-purpose flour
1 cup chopped pecans
1 cup raisins

Mix ingredients together in a large bowl. Pour into a greased 9x13-inch pan. Bake at 350° for 35-40 minutes or until toothpick inserted into center comes out clean. Cool and cut into squares.
Serves: 12-15

Origin: Mrs. Doris (Alice) Hebert
Favorite recipe of: Doris Hebert, Trainer, Abbeville, Louisiana
Career Highlights: Being leading Trainer at Evangeline Downs, Lafayette, Louisiana and Jefferson Downs, Kenner, Louisiana.

TRIPLE CROWN COCONUT CAKE

1 box white cake mix
¼ cup oil
3 eggs
8-ounce carton sour cream
1 8½-ounce can coconut cream
Frosting:
8-ounce package cream cheese
2 tablespoons milk
1 box powdered sugar
1 teaspoon vanilla
1 cup grated coconut

Mix all cake ingredients together at medium speed about 4 minutes. Pour into greased and floured 9x13-inch pan or 3 round layer pans. Bake at 350° for 30 minutes.
Frosting: Soften cream cheese and mix with all frosting ingredients. Spread on cooled cake.
Serves: 12-15

Origin: Mrs. Larry (Becky) Melancon
Favorite recipe of: Larry Melancon, Jockey, Louisville, Kentucky

STRAWBERRY CAKE

1 small box strawberry Jello
½ cup boiling water
4 eggs
½ cup butter-flavored oil
1 box yellow cake mix
2 cups fresh, sliced strawberries
1 box powdered sugar

Dissolve Jello in boiling water; cool. Beat eggs, oil, cooled Jello with cake mix. Beat until creamy, fold in 1 cup strawberries. Grease and flour tube pan or 9x13-inch pan. Bake in 350° oven for 45-60 minutes. For glaze, mix remaining 1 cup strawberries with powdered sugar. Juice from strawberries may be added to reach desired consistency. Pour over warm cake.
Serves: 12

Favorite recipe of: Larry Snyder, Jockey, Hot Springs, Arkansas
Career Highlights: Hall of fame rider who has won over 5,000 races.

"Pace — The speed of the leaders at each stage of the race."

PINEAPPLE UPSIDE-DOWN CAKE

½ cup butter
½ box dark brown sugar
1 can sliced pineapple
Maraschino cherries
1 box golden vanilla cake mix

Preheat oven to 350°. In an iron skillet, approximately 12-inch diameter, melt butter. Pour brown sugar into skillet and mix with fork. Remove from heat and place pineapple slices around in skillet with one in the center. Place a cherry in center of each pineapple. Set aside. Prepare cake mix according to package directions. Pour cake mix over pineapples. Bake in 350° oven for 40-45 minutes. When done, cool for 5 minutes then turn onto cake plate so that pineapples are on top. Can also be prepared and baked in 9x13-inch baking dish.
Serves: 8-10

Favorite recipe of: Leroy Moyers, Jockey, Cicero, Illinois

OWNER-TRAINER
PINEAPPLE DELIGHT CAKE

1 box white cake mix
1 20-ounce can crushed pineapple
1 4-ounce box instant vanilla or pineapple pudding mix
1 13-ounce container frozen whipped topping

Prepare cake according to directions on box. Pour into four 9-inch cake pans to make 4 thin layers. Let cool. Mix pineapple with pudding mix and fold into thawed whipped topping. Spread mixture between layers and on top of cake. Refrigerate 2 hours before serving. "Cool and not too sweet; men love it! Delicious with hot coffee after the races."
Serves: 10-12

Origin: Friends in Lafayette, Louisiana
Favorite recipe of: Revella Norman, Thoroughbred Owner, Bossier City, Louisiana
Career Highlights: Wife of Trainer, Gene Norman, mother of two sons, Cody and Cole Norman; co-founder of Racing Auxiliary of Louisiana; State President and Evangelin Downs chapter President, two terms; Super Derby Steering Committee; HBPA Board of Directors, Finance Chairperson.

"Filly — Female horse, aged four or less."

PEOPLE LIKE CARROTS TOO CAKE

1½ cups oil
2 cups sugar
3 eggs
1 cup drained crushed pineapple
1½ cups grated carrots
¼ cup coconut
¼ cup raisins
2½ cups flour
1 teaspoon baking soda
½ teaspoon salt
1 teaspoon cinnamon
1 teaspoon vanilla
1 cup chopped nuts
Topping:
1 box powdered sugar
6 tablespoons butter, softened
1 teaspoon vanilla
4 ounces cream cheese, softened

Cream oil, sugar and eggs in mixing bowl. Add pineapple, carrots, coconut and raisins. In separate bowl, sift flour, soda, salt and cinnamon. Add to carrot mixture and mix well. Stir in vanilla and nuts. When well mixed, pour into prepared bundt pan. Bake in preheated 350° oven for 1 hour or until toothpick inserted into center comes out clean. Let cool and remove from pan.
Topping: Combine all topping ingredients and mix well. Frost on cold cake.
Serves: 10-12

Favorite recipe of: Terry Mason, Trainer, Hot Springs, Arkansas
Racing interests: After working as Assistant Trainer under Bill Mott for 2 years and
under Larry Edwards for 1½ years, Terry is now a licensed trainer
working at Canterbury Downs with a stable of horses for
Rusty Arnold II.

YUM YUM CAKE

2 cups sugar
3 eggs
2 teaspoons soda
2 cups crushed pineapple
2 cups flour
Icing:
1 cup sugar
1 cup nuts
1 cup coconut
½ cup margarine
1 small can evaporated milk
1 teaspoon vanilla

Combine sugar, eggs, soda, pineapple and flour for cake. Mix well and pour into 9x13-inch pan. Bake at 350° for 40-45 minutes. Frost immediately with icing.
Icing: Boil sugar, margarine and milk for 2 minutes. Remove from heat and add remaining ingredients. Mix well and pour over cake while hot.
Serves: 12-15

Favorite recipe of: Bennett Parke, Director of Racing, Detroit Race Course,
Livonia, Michigan

OAKLAWN SYRUP CAKE

4 cups flour
2 cups Steen's syrup
1 cup sugar
2 teaspoons baking soda
1 cup milk
1 teaspoon vanilla
1 egg
1 cup chopped pecans, optional

Measure flour; add syrup, sugar, baking soda to flour. Combine milk, vanilla and beaten egg. Mix flour and milk mixtures until well blended. Add pecans if desired. Pour into 9x13-inch pan or muffin tins that have been greased. Bake at 350° until center is cooked, about 30-35 minutes.
Serves: 20-24

Origin: Mrs. Bob's, Hot Springs, Arkansas, "When making our yearly trip to Oaklawn
Park in March, Mrs. Bob always made our crowd a recipe of these syrup cakes."
Favorite recipe of: Janet P. Stemmans, "Tack Lady", Stemmans, Inc.,
Carencro, Louisiana

PISTACHIO CAKE

1 box yellow cake mix
3 small boxes pistachio pudding mix
½ cup water
½ cup oil
5 eggs
1 cup milk, divided
⅔ container (9-ounce) frozen whipped topping

Mix dry ingredients: cake mix and 2 boxes pudding mix. Add water, oil, ½ cup milk and 1 egg at a time. After all eggs have been beaten into the mixture, beat 4 more minutes. Pour into greased and floured tube or bundt pan. Bake at 350° for 50 minutes. Frosting: Blend together 1 remaining box of pudding, remaining ½ cup milk and whipped topping. Beat until stiff. Frost on cool cake. Refrigerate.
Serves: 12

Origin: Mrs. Jack (Helen) Van Berg's friends Ms. Moore and Ms. Abshire, "One of Jack's favorite cakes and he would love it even more if you would double the frosting!!"
Favorite recipe of: Jack Van Berg, Owner-Trainer, Goschen, Kentucky
Career Highlights: Winner of the Eclipse Award as North America's champion trainer in 1984; in 1983, became the only American trainer to win 4,000 races; won his eighth national training title for most victories in 1984 with 258 wins, about $4.1 million in purses and his first classic race, the Preakness with *Gate Dancer.*

COMBINATION CHOCOLATE CAKE

1 box chocolate cake mix
1 21-ounce can cherry pie filling
3 eggs, beaten
Frosting: 2 cups sugar
½ cup butter
⅔ cup milk
1 12-ounce package chocolate chips

Mix eggs and pie filling into cake mix. Mix well and pour into 9x13-inch greased cake pan. Bake at 350° for 30-35 minutes. Cool. Frosting: In a saucepan, combine sugar, butter and milk. Bring to a boil, stir and continue to boil for 1½ minutes. Remove from heat, add chocolate chips and beat until smooth. Frost on cool cake. Freezes very well.
Serves: 12-15

Favorite recipe of: Mrs. J. J. (Joan) Pletcher, Thoroughbred Owner, Benton, Louisiana

"Combination — Across-the-board bet for which a single mutuel ticket is issued."

BLACK GOLD CHOCOLATE CAKE

6 tablespoons cocoa, unsweetened
1 cup water
2 cups sugar
½ cup butter
2 egg yolks
2½ cups flour
1 cup buttermilk
2 teaspoons baking soda
¼ teaspoon salt
1 teaspoon vanilla
2 egg whites

Boil cocoa and water for 5 minutes until slightly thick. Cream sugar, butter and egg yolks. Sift together flour, soda and salt and add to sugar-butter mixture, alternating buttermilk with dry ingredients. Add vanilla and cocoa mixture. Fold in stiffly beaten egg whites. Pour into 2 greased and floured round cake pans or 1 oblong cake pan. Bake at 375° for 20-30 minutes. Test with toothpick for doneness. The secret to this cake is not to overbake. Cool and frost with following French Butter Cream Frosting.

FRENCH BUTTER CREAM FROSTING

2 cups sugar
½ cup water
⅛ teaspoon salt
¼ teaspoon cream of tartar
4 egg whites
2-3 cups powdered sugar
1½ teaspoons vanilla
4 tablespoons soft butter
Optional: 4 squares unsweetened chocolate for Chocolate Frosting

Place sugar, water, salt and cream of tartar in a saucepan over medium heat, stirring just long enough until clear, then boil without stirring until mixture reaches 260°. Set aside and cool. Beat egg whites until stiff and add cooled syrup mixture slowly. Beat 3 minutes. At low speed, beat in 2 cups powdered sugar (may have to add a little more for desired consistency). Fold in vanilla and softened butter. If making Chocolate Frosting, melt squares over a double boiler and add to cooled syrup or add squares (cut up) to hot syrup mixture after it has reached 260°. Will frost two 9-inch round cakes.
Serves: 12-15

Origin: Frona Day Winegardner, Springfield, Missouri, "This recipe is a real favorite
     and has been in her use for over 70 years. Can be made ahead and frozen
     and then frosted."
Favorite recipe of: Sam Maple, Jockey, Hot Springs, Arkansas
Career Highlights: Being from Ohio, Sam remembers winning the Ohio Derby aboard
     Smarten on Father's Day with his Dad and family there.

NEVER FAIL CHOCOLATE CAKE

2 cups flour
2 cups sugar
½ cup butter
½ cup oil
¼ cup cocoa
1 cup water
½ cup buttermilk
1 teaspoon vanilla
1 teaspoon soda
2 eggs

In a large bowl, mix flour and sugar together. In a saucepan, combine butter, oil, cocoa and water. Bring to a boil and pour over flour and sugar. Mix until well blended. Add buttermilk, vanilla, soda and eggs. Beat until well mixed (mixture will be bubbly). Pour mixture into a well greased cookie sheet with ¼-inch sides. Bake at 400° for 20 minutes.
Serves: 12-15

Favorite recipe of: John Lively, Jockey, Pearcy, Arkansas
Career Highlights: Won the Preakness in 1976 on *Elocutionist;* won
Arlington-Washington Futurity on *Let's Don't Fight* in 1981; leading
rider at Ak-Sar-Ben, Omaha, Nebraska for eight years; leading rider
at Oaklawn Park, Hot Springs, Arkansas for two years.

ICING FOR
NEVER FAIL CHOCOLATE CAKE

½ cup margarine
3 heatping tablespoons cocoa
6 tablespoons milk
1 box powdered sugar, sifted
1 teaspoon vanilla
1 cup chopped pecans

While cake is baking, melt margarine in heavy saucepan. Add cocoa and milk and bring to a boil. Remove from heat and add powdered sugar and beat well. Add vanilla and pecans; beat again. Spread over warm cake.

Favorite recipe of: Larry Snyder, Jockey, Hot Springs, Arkansas
Career Highlights: Leading rider in the U.S. in 1969 with 352 wins; leading rider
at Oaklawn Park seven times, including three straight between
1980 and 1982; won his 4,000th career race at Louisiana Downs
in 1979 and his 5,000th career race again at Louisiana Downs
in 1984.

COCONUT CARMEL PECAN TART

Dough:
1½ cups all purpose flour
½ cup cake flour
½ cup unsalted butter, cut in pieces
⅓ cup sugar
1 egg yolk
⅓ cup cold water
Coconut Filling:
1 cup sugar
½ cup butter
½ cup whipping cream
2 eggs
7-ounce package coconut, shredded
7 ounces pecan pieces

Dough: Mix flours and sugar. Cut butter into flour until mixture looks like coarse meal. Add water and yolk and mix with fork just until moist. Turn out onto board and smear with palm of your hand piece by piece until well blended. Don't knead. Roll out on floured board and line 9-inch pie pan. Dough must be kept chilled while working or butter will soften and make it difficult to use. Line dough-lined pan with waxed paper and fill with dried beans. Put in 425° oven for 8-12 minutes, or until edges of dough turn golden brown (but not too brown). Remove waxed paper and beans and return to oven until dough is golden brown throughout, about 10-15 minutes. Cool and fill with Coconut Filling.
Coconut Filling: Mix sugar with ¼ cup water in saucepan and cook until golden brown carmel. Remove from heat and pour in cream gradually, swirling pan to dissolve caramel. Return to heat to finish dissolving. Remove from heat and add butter, swirling until melted. In a small bowl, wisk eggs and pour into saucepan all at once, wisking mixture constantly as you add eggs. Return to heat and continue wisking until mixture begins to simmer. Remove from heat and very quickly add coconut and pecans. Stir to blend and quickly pour into baked shell. Spread until smooth and let set for 2-3 hours. Do not refrigerate.
Serves: 8

Origin: Charles Cella, Hot Springs, Arkansas
Favorite recipe of: Erma Hicks, Horseman's Bookkeeper, Oaklawn Park and
Louisiana Downs

"Circuit — Geographical grouping of tracks whose meetings are coordinated to run in sequence."

JUDY COOPER

A working farm manager of her own Tree Line Thoroughbreds, Judy Cooper finds time for doing portraiture of her greatest passion, the Thoroughbred. Her work is included in the private collections of many distinguished owners, trainers, jockeys and race enthusiasts in the US and Canada.

Each year, Ms. Cooper paints the finish of the previous year's Super Derby race, with the original watercolor donated to the National Kidney Foundation of Louisiana, to be auctioned at the Super Derby-Kidney Foundation Ball. Proceeds from the painting go to this very deserving Foundation so that many will benefit from the race long after the cheers on Super Derby Day.

CREME DE ALMOND TORTE

2 envelopes unflavored gelatin
½ cup water
1 7-ounce jar marshmallow creme
½ cup melted butter
2 tablespoons water
6 eggs
8½-ounce package chocolate wafer cookies, crushed
⅓ cup sugar
¾ cup creme de almond liqueur
1½ cups whipping cream, whipped or 3 cups frozen whipped topping,
    thawed

In a small saucepan pour gelatin over ½ cup water. Over low heat, stir until dissolved. Cool. Combine crushed cookies and melted butter; set aside. Blend 2 tablespoons water and marshmallow creme. Separate eggs. Beat egg whites until stiff but not dry. Fold into marshmallow mixture. Beat sugar and egg yolks until thick. Fold egg yolk mixture, liqueur, whipped cream and gelatin into egg white mixture. Spoon ¼ the almond mixture (1 ⅓ cups) into a 12-cup tube pan. Sprinkle with ¾ cup crushed cookies. Carefully spoon ½ remaining almond mixture over crumbs. Sprinkle with 1 cup crumbs. Spoon on remaining almond mixture and crumbs. Press lightly and freeze. Recipe may be halved for 6-cup tube pan.
Serves: 10-12

Favorite recipe of: Mr. and Mrs. Blanton W. Cooper, Tree Line Farm,
         Elm Grove, Louisiana

TORTE DI NOCHE

½ cup soft butter
⅔ cup sugar
1 egg, room temperature
1 cup finely chopped walnuts
1 teaspoon grated lemon rind
1½ teaspoon baking powder
1 cup sifted flour
3-4 tablespoons light rum

Butter bottom of 9-inch pan with removable sides. Dust with flour. Cream butter, sugar and egg. In a separate bowl combine walnuts, lemon rind, baking powder and flour. Fold two mixtures together. Add rum. Bake in a 350° oven for 30-35 minutes.
"Excellent with coffee after the races!"
Serves: 6

Origin: Mrs. Pat (Jeanne) Pope, Bossier City, Louisiana
Favorite recipe of: Patrick J. Pope, Racing Secretary, Louisiana
         Downs, Bossier City, Louisiana

EXPRESSO TORTE

4 teaspoons instant coffee powder
1 tablespoon hot water
4 eggs, separated
½ cup sugar
1 cup heavy cream
3 tablespoons coffee flavored liqueur (Kahlua)

Dissolve coffee powder in hot water and set aside. Beat egg whites until stiff, then gradually add sugar, beating until whites hold short glossy peaks. Fold in coffee liquid and set aside. Beat egg yolks until thick and light in color; set aside. Whip cream until stiff and blend in liqueur. Thoroughly fold whites, yolks, and cream together and pour into springform pan lined with graham crust. Cover and freeze until firm, 8 hours or longer. Remove pan sides, set torte on serving dish, top with nuts, cut in wedges.

GRAHAM CRUST

1 cup finely crushed graham cracker crumbs
2 tablespoons melted butter
3 tablespoons sugar
¼ cup finely chopped nuts, almonds or walnuts
Additional nuts for top

Blend graham cracker crumbs with butter, sugar and chopped nuts. Pat evenly over bottom of 8 or 9-inch pan (2 inches deep) with removable bottom or spring released sides.
Serves: 8-10

Origin: Leigh Lawrence, Cambria, California
Favorite recipe of: Mrs. Louis (Nita) Brooks, Thoroughbred Owner, Sweetwater, Texas

MARYDEL'S KEY LIME PIE

10-inch Graham cracker crust, follow the directions on box.
6 egg yolks
1½ cans sweetened condensed milk
6-8 ounces fresh squeezed Florida Key limes (no substitutes)
Whipped cream

Beat egg yolks slightly and add condensed milk and blend thoroughly. Add lime juice slowly and mix well. Pour into cooled pie shell. Refrigerate for several hours before serving. Top with whipped cream.
Serves: 8

Favorite recipe of: Mary R. Odom, Owner, Marydel Farm, Middletown, Delaware

ARCHIE'S CHESS PIE

1 9-inch pie crust, unbaked
2 cups sugar
4 whole eggs
¼ cup cream or milk
1 tablespoon lemon juice
Pinch salt
1 teaspoon vanilla
2 teaspoon corn meal
¼ cup butter, melted and browned

Mix together all ingredients, adding butter last. Mix well and pour into pie shell. Bake at 350° for about 1 hour, or until solid when shook.
Yield: 1 9-inch pie

Favorite recipe of: Archie Lofton, Thoroughbred Owner, Wichita Falls, Texas

CHOCOLATE CHESS PIE

1 9-inch unbaked pastry shell
¼ cup butter or margarine
1½ 1-ounce squares unsweetened chocolate, melted with butter
1½ cups sugar
1 tablespoon flour
2 eggs
½ cup evaporated milk
1 teaspoon vanilla
Few grains salt

Pour melted butter and chocolate mixture into small mixer bowl. Add remaining ingredients and beat at moderate speed for 6 minutes. Pour mixture into pastry shell. Bake in preheated 350° oven for 40 minutes. Filling will be puffy and will fall as it cools. Serve cold. May be topped with whipped cream or ice cream.
Serves: 6-8

Favorite recipe of: Mr. and Mrs. Theodore R. Kuster, Paris, Kentucky
Career Highlights: Ted Kuster is Owner-Manager of Westview Farm, thoroughbred breeding operaton; past president Kentucky Thoroughbred Farm Managers Club; T.C.A.; breeder of several stake winners.

"Stud fee — What the stallion's owner gets for its breeding services."

PARI-MUTUEL PECAN PIE

¼ cup butter
½ cup sugar
½ cup brown sugar
1 cup light corn syrup
¼ teaspoon salt
1 tablespoon flour
2-3 eggs
1 cup whole or chopped pecans

Cream butter and sugars. Add syrup, salt and flour. Mix with beaten eggs. Mix together for 3 minutes. Pour into unbaked 9-inch pie shell (recipe follows). Bake at 400° for 10 minutes, then reduce heat to 325° and bake for an additional 45 minutes.

PIE CRUST
(for two 9-inch pie shells)

2 cups flour
⅔ cup shortening
1 egg, beaten
4 tablespoons ice water
1 tablespoon vinegar

Cut shortening into flour with a fork until mixture resembles coarse crumbs. Mix water and egg together and add to flour mixture. Sprinkle vinegar over mixture until it is just moist enough to gather into a ball. Divide dough in half and roll out on floured surface or pastry cloth. Pie crust can be frozen until ready to use.

Origin: Pie filling recipe is from Mrs. Sam (Jill) Maple
　　　　Crust recipe is from Lottie Jester, Hot Springs, Arkansas
Favorite recipe of: Sam Maple, Jockey, Hot Springs, Arkansas
Career Highlights:　Sam won six stakes races in a row, including graded stakes,
　　　　Bewitched, Hempstead and Apple Blossom on *Heatherten*,
　　　　owned by John Franks and trained by Bill Mott.

"Pari-mutuel — From Paris ("Paree") Mutuels, system invented by Frenchman, whereby winning bettors get all money wagered by losers, after deduction of house percentage."

ROLLED PECAN PIE

½ cup margarine
1 cup sugar
3 tablespoons flour
1 cup milk
3 egg yolks
1 tablespoon vanilla
1 cup pecans
1 9-inch baked pie shell

*In a saucepan over medium heat, melt butter. Add sugar and flour and stir
well. Beat egg yolks into milk and add to saucepan. Continue cooking until
mixture thickens. Add vanilla and nuts and pour into baked pie shell. Top
with sweetened whipped cream.*
Serves: 8

Favorite recipe of: Mr. and Mrs. Phil Like, Thoroughbred Owners, Dalhart, Texas

LUCKY LARRY'S LUSCIOUS PIE

2 eggs
1 cup sugar
1 13-ounce can evaporated milk
1 6-ounce package chocolate pudding mix
½ cup margarine
2 teaspoons vanilla
1 9-inch baked pie shell

*Beat eggs; add sugar, milk and pudding mix (not instant). Cook slowly until
thick and remove from heat. Add margarine and stir until melted. Add vanilla
and cool. Pour into baked pie shell.*

NO WEEP MERINGUE

3 egg whites
Dash salt
1 cup marshmallow creme

*Beat whites with salt until soft peaks form. Add marshmallow creme and
beat again until soft peaks return. Spread over filling and seal edges. Bake
at 350° for 12-15 minutes. Refrigerate.*
Yield: One 9-inch pie

Origin: Mrs. Larry (Becky) Melancon
Favorite recipe of: Larry Melancon, Jockey, Louisville, Kentucky
Career Highlights: Rider of *Come Summer,* winner of the first running of the
                Canterbury Derby, Canterbury Downs, Spakopee, Minnesota.

HEAVENLY PIE

4 eggs
2 cups milk
¾ cup sugar
½ cup flour
¼ cup butter or margarine, softened
Dash of salt
1 teaspoon vanilla
1 cup coconut

Put all ingredients in blender as given. Turn blender on high speed and count to 10 slowly. Turn off blender and pour into a well greased 10-inch pie plate. Bake for 40 minutes at 350°. It makes its own crust and tastes like a custard pie.
Serves: 6-8

Origin: Mrs. Steve (Mary Jo) Gasper
Favorite recipe of: Mr. and Mrs. Steve Gasper, Omaha, Nebraska
Career Highlights: Former managers of Walmac Farm in Lexington, Kentucky. Parents of John J. Gasper who works as a Jockey Agent in Lexington.

FUTURITY FUDGE PIE

½ cup flour
1 cup sugar
½ cup butter
1 square unsweetened chocolate
2 eggs
1 teaspoon vanilla
¾ cup chopped pecans
1 8-inch unbaked pie shell

Melt butter and chocolate together, add sugar and beat well. Add eggs, 1 at a time. Beat in flour and vanilla. Fold in pecans and pour into unbaked pie shell. Bake at 350° for 30 minutes or until set. Serve warm with ice cream or whipped cream.
Note: For 9-inch pie shell, make 1½ recipe and bake 10 minutes longer.
Yield: One 8 or 9-inch pie

Origin: Amelda L. Wiggins, Haughton, Louisiana
Favorite recipe of: Randy Romero, Jockey, Bossier City, Louisiana
Career Highlights: Set a state record in Louisiana for wins at one meeting with 181 victories at the 1983-84 Fair Grounds meeting; won second straight Fair Grounds title in 1984-85; two-time riding champion at Louisiana Downs, 1979 and 1980; one of only two jockeys to ride in both the Kentucky Derby and the All-American Futurity; Captured the 1984 Ruffian Handicap at Belmont Park and the Ladies Handicap at Aqueduct aboard *Heatherten*.

LOUIE'S POTLUCK PUMPKIN PIE

1 cup sugar
¼ teaspoon salt
½ teaspoon ground ginger
1 teaspoon cinnamon
½ teaspoon nutmeg
½ teaspoon ground cloves
1 16-ounce can pumpkin
1 8-ounce carton sour cream
3 eggs, separated
1 unbaked 9-inch pastry shell (or as we prefer, graham cracker crust)
Whipped cream

Combine first 6 ingredients; add pumpkin and sour cream, stirring well. Beat egg yolks until thick and lemon colored and stir into pumpkin mixture. Beat egg whites (at room temperature) until stiff peaks form; fold into pumpkin mixture. Note: You might want to taste mixture to see if you prefer more nutmeg or cinnamon. Pour into pastry shell and bake at 450° for 10 minutes. Reduce heat to 350° and bake for 55 minutes or until set. Top each serving with whipped cream.
Another note from contributor, Vic Heerman: "I often double the spice content, but Louie suggests some people are not as fond of spices as I am. 'Make one and you be the butcher,' as they say at the track! Louie has often used a pumpkin pie spice in addition to above. Also a dash of vanilla extract; anything to add to flavor pumpkin we find."
Serves: 8

Origin: Mrs. Victor (Louie) Heerman, Jr.
Favorite recipe of: Victor Heerman, Jr., Heerman Bloodstock Agency, Lexington, Kentucky.
Career Highlights: "I guess I came nearest to fame by planning the mating for, foaling, raising, and selling of *Spectacular Bid.* The next year, I foaled, raised, and sold the Epsom Derby Winner, *Golden Fleece.* Some years before, I had been responsible for the mating which produced the first California millionaire, *Native Diver,* winner of 34 stakes from 36 wins in all."

"Graded race — One in which eligibility is limited to horses in one or another classification, as determined by racing secretary. Graded allowances and graded handicaps are common."

PIE WITH A KICK

1 9-inch pie shell, unbaked
1 cup semi-sweet chocolate chips
½ cup butter
2 eggs, slightly beaten
1 cup sugar
1 cup pecans
2 tablespoons GOOD KENTUCKY BOURBON

Line pie shell with semi-sweet chocolate chips. Melt butter and mix with eggs, sugar, pecans and bourbon. Pour mixture over chocolate chips and bake for 30-35 minutes at 350°. Garnish with fresh mint and enjoy!
Serves: 8

Origin: Mrs. Alyce Relford, Lexington, Kentucky
Favorite recipe of: Howard L. Battle, Lexington, Kentucky
Career Highlights: Racing Secretary since 1967, currently at Keeneland;
owner of Hoofprints which deals in Battle's equine
prints and greeting cards.

QUINELLA FIG COOKIES

2½ cups sugar
3 eggs
1 cup shredded coconut
1 teaspoon baking powder
½ teaspoon nutmeg
¾ cup butter
2 cups fig preserves
2 cups chopped pecans
1 teaspoon cinnamon
3½ cups all-purpose flour
1 cup raisins

Mix ingredients together well. Drop dough from teaspoon, larger if desired, onto baking sheet. Bake at 350° for 15-20 minutes or until brown.
Yield: About 6 dozen cookies, depending on size.

Origin: Mrs. Doris (Alice) Hebert
Favorite recipe of: Doris Hebert, Trainer, Abbeville, Louisiana

"Quinella — Form of mutuel betting in which player tries to pick first two finishers, regardless of order."

FARRAH'S FAVORITE CHOCOLATE COOKIES

½ cup vegetable oil
4 ounces unsweetened chocolate, melted
2 cups sugar
4 eggs
2 teaspoons vanilla
2 cups sifted flour
2 teaspoons baking powder
½ teaspoons salt
1 cup powdered sugar

Mix oil, chocolate and sugar. Blend in 1 egg at a time. Add vanilla, flour, baking powder, salt and mix well. Chill several hours or overnight. Make balls using 1 teaspoon dough. Roll in powdered sugar and place on greased cookie sheet about 2 inches apart. Bake in preheated 350° oven for 10-12 minutes. Do not overbake. Can be frozen after rolled in sugar and baked later.
Yield: About 7 dozen cookies.

Origin: "A cousin in Texas sent this recipe to me."
Favorite recipe of: Farrah Fawcett, Actress and Thoroughbred Racing Enthusiast
Los Angeles, California

PEANUT BUTTER COOKIES

1 cup flour
½ teaspoon soda
¼ teaspoon salt
½ cup shortening, soft
½ cup brown sugar, packed
½ cup white sugar
1 egg, unbeaten
½ cup peanut butter
1 tablespoon water
½ teaspoon vanilla

Sift together flour, soda and salt. In large bowl combine remaining ingredients. Beat well then add flour mixture. Drop by rounded teaspoon on cookie sheet. Press a criss-cross design lightly on top of cookie with a fork that has been dipped in water. Bake at 325° for 12-18 minutes.
Yield: 5-6 dozen

Origin: Joy Cobena, Metairie, Louisiana
Favorite recipe of: The Editor

MAPLE'S MAISINA COOKIES

1 14-ounce can condensed milk
1 pound butter
1½ cups sugar
3 egg yolks
1 egg
1 teaspoon vanilla
1 lime
1 jigger cognac
3½-4 cups corn starch
1-1½ cups flour
1 teaspoon baking soda
2 teaspoons baking powder
½ cup shredded coconut

Boil unopened can condensed milk in a saucepan of water for 2½-3 hours. This turns into a thick caramel. Mix butter and sugar until creamy and add beaten yolks and beaten egg. Mix in vanilla, cognac and all the juice of the squeezed lime. Sift dry ingredients together, saving ½ cup each of the corn starch and flour. Combine sugar-butter mixture with flour mixture adding the extra corn starch and flour if necessary to be able to knead. Knead 5-10 minutes, then roll out to ¼-½ inch thickness. Cut cookies with shot glass and place on buttered baking sheet. Bake at 350° until golden, about 7-10 minutes, then let cool. Frost 1 cookie with condensed milk and top with another cookie to make a sandwich. Push together enough to squeeze a little frosting out, then roll in coconut. "These are time consuming but boy are they great! Perfect for holidays and gifts."

Origin: Mrs. Sam (Jill) Maple obtained this recipe from the hostess of the house where
she and Sam stayed on their honeymoon in 1975, Ninon Pardo,
Guarujah, Brazil.
Favorite recipe of: Sam Maple, Jockey, Hot Springs, Arkansas
Career Highlights: Winning Omaha Gold Cup in two consecutive years with
Joachim in 1976 and *Jatski* in 1977; competing in the All-Star
Jockey races at Hollywood Park in 1977.

"Sit-still — A type of riding dependent more on patience, knowledge of pace than active, 'Whoop-de-doo' whipping; of a jockey who loses the race through inactivity with the whip."

MELTING MINUTES TO POST
(Cookies)

1 cup butter, softened
5½ tablespoons powdered sugar
¾ cup cornstarch
1 cup flour
Icing:
1 cup powdered sugar
1 tablespoon butter
1 tablespoon milk
1½ teaspoons vanilla

Mix cookie ingredients together until well blended. Drop by rounded teaspoon onto cookie sheet. Bake at 350° for 12-15 minutes or until light in color, brown on top.
Icing: Mix icing ingredients together well. Spread on warm cookies.
Yield: About 3 dozen cookies.

Favorite recipe of: Joe King, Trainer, Louisville, Kentucky

"Shut out — What happens to the player who gets on the betting line too late and is still waiting in line when the window closes."

Sir Barton 1919

Gallant Fox 1930

Omaha 1935

War Admiral 1937

Whirlaway 1941

Count Fleet 1943

Assault 1946

Citation 1948

Secretarial 1973

Triple
Crown
Winners

Seattle Slew 1977

Affirmed 1978

TRIPLE CROWN SERIES
By Howard L. Battle

Howard L. Battle is a third generation horseman and professional equine artist. He has been a Racing Secretary since 1967; Detroit Race Course; started thoroughbred racing in Pennsylvania; Delaware Park; AkSarBen; Churchill Downs and currently at Keeneland. He received a Master's Degree in Fine Arts from Notre Dame. Battle paints numerous commissioned Thoroughbred portraits and owns Hoofprints which deals in equine prints and greeting cards.

Howard Battle has generously allowed PROVEN PERFORMANCES to begin the section "Triple Crown Winners" with his lovely sketches of the eleven Triple Crown winners entitled "Triple Crown Series".

Triple Crown Winners

"The Kentucky Derby"

"The Preakness"

"The Belmont"

Editor's Note: Ellen Parker has composed a series of recipes for *Proven Performances* she has entitled TRIPLE CROWN WINNERS. It was so beautifully done that I left the entire composition intact, so I will let Ellen begin.

TRIPLE CROWN WINNERS

Each year as April passes into May, thousands of hopes have been realized or dashed. A promising two year old who did not develop, and the less precocious one who did. The last minute injury of a champion, the late development of another. Each horseman has a common goal, whether he's based in Seattle or Kentucky. Each owner, breeder, rider and groom. That goal is to win the Triple Crown.

These three races — The Kentucky Derby, The Preakness and The Belmont Stakes are, indeed, the crown jewels of turfdom. A win in any brings honor, a win in two a probable championship; a victory in each immortality.

Many of us are unable to personally attend each of the races, but I have begun a tradition in my home that brings me a little closer as I watch with anticipation for another *Seattle Slew* or *Secretariat* to flash across my television screen. Thus, I bring the cooking of Louisville, Baltimore, New York, into our lives for those all important Saturdays. You may wish to begin a similar tradition. And you don't have to limit yourself to the Triple Crown - how about a Salmon Souffle for The Longacres Mile? Or a beef stroganoff made with some of that special Chicago beef for the Arlington Million.

For as surely as the blades of the Bluegrass spell Thoroughbred, good food cooked for a special occasion spells love. In this case it is two-fold; love for your special friends and family, and a celebration of the Champions.

"THE KENTUCKY DERBY"

No Kentucky Derby party would be complete without a big pot of Burgoo bubbling on the stove. Burgoo can be made the night before the big race and cooked slowly in a crock pot. The next morning can then be kept free to relax and prepare for the company you will surely want to invite; Burgoo feeds a lot of people, although it can be frozen.

SLEW BURGOO

3 large chicken breasts
2 small steaks, tenderized and cubed
1 pound veal, cubed
2 tablespoons bacon fat
3 large onions, chopped
3 cloves garlic, minced
2 bunches celery tops, chopped
½ cup chopped parsley
1 red pepper, chopped or pimentos, well drained and chopped
1 bay leaf
1 tablespoon fresh ground pepper
Salt to taste
4 medium carrots, sliced
2 small or 1 large turnip, diced
3 stalks celery, diced
½ cup sliced okra
3 large potatoes, diced
¼ head cabbage, chopped and sauteed in butter
½ cup fresh or frozen greens, chopped
½ can black eyed peas
½ cup corn, fresh off the cob is best
1 15-ounce can stewed tomatoes
2 tablespoons thyme
Dash Tabasco
1 cup red wine
¼ cup GOOD Kentucky Bourbon

Cut chicken in chunks and saute in bacon fat. Add to crock pot. Then add remaining ingredients in order given through the Tabasco. Add wine to keep semi-solid and cook on slow heat overnight. In the morning, taste, adjust seasonings and add bourbon (I prefer Maker's Mark). Burgoo is a meal in itself, but for the hungry men, hot biscuits or cornbread is an added filler.
Serves: A Crowd

THE MINT JULIP

No Kentucky Derby party would be complete without a real Mint Julip. The secret is to drink them WITH your Burgoo, or go easy before as this "Bluegrass Nectar" has a tendency to sneak up on one.

The first essential for this is the best bourbon you can buy. Maker's Mark again is best, but Ezra Brooks or Early Times will do nicely as well. In a pinch, go ahead and use Jack Daniels, but it's TENNESSEE whiskey!

Make certain ahead of time that you have on hand a large amount of crushed ice. Everyone is going to want more than one, and it's frustrating to keep overworking the blender while the guests take on a pleasant glow.

Two kinds of mint are required — spearmint and peppermint. Fresh in both cases — or grow your own in a window box, they flourish in a small planter. Mash one sugar cube with a little VERY COLD water (preferably refrigerated water — branch water if you can get it) and then mash in some of the peppermint leaves. Fill the glass with the shaved ice and allow it to frost a moment. Fill to the brim with the bourbon and garnish with the spearmint after lightly rubbing it around the rim of the glass. A dash of 151 rum is optional, but I'm a purist.

If Burgoo doesn't strike your fancy (although I can't imagine it NOT doing so), here's a real down home Kentucky supper that might do the trick:

BLUEGRASS SUPPER SUPREME

The night before, marinate ham steaks in apple juice, just enough to cover. Both of these other dishes can be made the evening before:

ROSE'S CHEESE GRITS

1 cup quick cooking grits
4 cups water
1 teaspoon salt
3 tablespoons butter
1 cup shredded Cheddar cheese
Dash Tabasco
1 cup milk
Additional shredded Cheddar for topping
Parmesan cheese for topping

Cook grits in salted water according to package directions. Combine with remaining ingredients and turn into buttered casserole. Cover with additional Cheddar cheese and sprinkle with Parmesan cheese. Bake at 375° for 45 minutes. Optional additions to this creamy, satisfying dish are onion flakes or garlic salt. If made the evening before and refrigerated, bring to room temperature before baking.

BLACK EYED PEAS YOU'LL NEVER MAKE FUN OF

The humble black eyed pea gets a lot of play in Southern jokes and old Tennessee Williams movies, but I've found a way to dress up that staple of the South so that even a Yankee would enjoy it.

Again, this may be prepared the evening before, then brought to room temperature and heated.

2½ tablespoons butter
2-4 green onions, depending on size
1 small stalk celery
1 large can black eyed peas
2 slices Canadian bacon
2 teaspoons sugar
½ tablespoon marjoram
¼ tablespoon white pepper

In a saucepan, melt the butter and add the chopped onion and celery and saute. Put the peas in a baking dish and add sauteed onion and celery. Saute chopped slices of Canadian bacon sprinkled with sugar to brown well and add to the peas along with the browned bits from the pan. Add marjoram and pepper; stir mixture well.

When warming, this need only warm through. You may wish to add it to the oven the last 5-7 minutes of baking the cheese grits and then allow it to sit while the grits cool.

HAM-LOVERS HEAVEN
"Ham Steaks with Red-Eye Gravy"

The very first thing I ever ate in Kentucky was ham. Perhaps I am merely keeping a memory alive, but I contend to this day that that was the best ham I have ever eaten. Obviously, somewhere along the line it was necessary for me to figure out a way to duplicate that ham. I think I've finally managed to succeed.

Ham steaks marinated in apple juice
Butter
Sugar
Flour
Chicken stock

Drain ham slices that have marinated overnight in apple juice. Heat skillet; add two tablespoons butter or more may be added as you cook. Add ham steaks sprinkled with sugar (to brown) and continue to saute until almost crispy on outside. Keep warm on heated platter. To mixture and drippings in pan, add enough butter to scrape up all the good brown bits and add flour, slowly, a little at a time until mixture thickens. Add chicken stock until gravy reaches desired thickness (red-eye gravy shouldn't be TOO thick) and serve immediately with your bubbling cheese grits and black eyed peas. Hot biscuits or cornbread may, of course, be added to the menu.

If everyone isn't too full for dessert, a light and simple last course is champagne poured over lime sherbet.

"THE PREAKNESS"
ON TO BALTIMORE

I've never been to Baltimore, though I've always wanted to go, just as I've wanted to tour the farms in the beautiful countryside and see *Norther Dancer* in person just once, *Kelso's* home, and the birthplace of a mare I once owned. I have, however, several good friends from this part of the world and clams and crab seem a fitting menu for anyone who enjoys good horses — and good food.

My first recipe, Linguine with Clam Sauce, is a personal creation, one I'm rather proud of in fact. It's gotten compliments from those two Maryland-born friends, so it is now a staple of Preakness Day in the Parker household:

PRONOUNCED GOOD BY AN ITALIAN NUN
"Linguine with Clam Sauce"

1 small yellow onion, finely chopped
2 small stalks celery, finely chopped
½ cup sweet butter, approximately
1 small can sliced mushrooms, drained
1 head roasted garlic*
1 15-ounce can peeled tomatoes, drained (retain juice)
1 medium can baby clams, drained (retain juice)
Salt and pepper, to taste
2-3 tablespoons flour
Pinch oregano
2 cloves fresh garlic, minced
1 16-ounce package linguine, regular or spinach
Romano cheese, freshly grated

To roast garlic (mild flavor, good texture) brush with olive oil and wrap tightly in foil. Bake at 350° for 10-15 minutes. Cool. Cloves will slip out of skins. Peel and set aside.

Saute onion and celery in two tablespoons butter until limp but not golden. Add minced, roasted garlic, tomatoes and clams. Season with salt and pepper. In saucepan, melt 3-4 tablespoons butter and add flour to thicken slightly. Add juice of clams and tomatoes, oregano and the fresh, minced garlic cloves. Simmer until sauce is somewhat reduced in volume. Add tomato and clam mixture and simmer 30-45 minutes. (Use stock to thin or flour to thicken if necessary.) In meantime, prepare linguine. Toss with butter, salt and pepper. Pour sauce overall and serve at once. Top with fresh grated Romano cheese.

There is, of course, but one proper accompaniment to such hearty fair — a mixed leaf lettuce salad with a light oil and vinegar dressing. French bread, preferably heated, is also welcome with this meal.

For any heavy dinner such as this, or for any seafood, such as the steamed clams which will follow, I find the following a marvelous light beverage.

LEMONY WHITE WINE

Your favorite dry, white wine (I enjoy Pouilly Fuisse)
Fresh lemons

Chill wine glasses which have been rinsed with the juice of a lemon; add your favorite white wine; garnish with chilled lemon wedge.

Steamed clams may seem an ordinary dish to many, but they seem to me, served with a bowl of their hearty broth and hot French bread to be almost soothing.

CITATION CLAMS

Clams should be steamed in the following solution — depending upon the number of your guests, you may wish to increase the portions, but it is important to have enough broth from the clams to ensure good 'dipping' with the hot bread.

The Solution: 1 part white wine to 1 part stock to 1 part clam juice in proportions large enough to cover the amount of clams to be cooked. Add to solution 2 cloves minced garlic, a dash of white pepper and 1 tablespoon butter to enrich sauce. Place well scrubbed clams in broth or on a steamer rack if you prefer and cook until each opens fully. Discard any clams that do not open.

Serve with a portion of the broth for each person, plus drawn butter for dipping if desired. And don't forget that all important hot bread which will be very valuable indeed when your guests discover that clam broth.
The dessert, like the wine, should once again be light. Peach or champagne sherbet compliments clams with a hearty flavor nicely.

"THE BELMONT"
THE CULMINATION

Belmont Park. Scene of the final Triple Crown race. If one horse has captured the first two jewels in the series, everyone may be too excited to eat until AFTER the race.
You might want to begin with some appetizers:

BROILED WATER CHESTNUTS

Water chestnuts wrapped in half a bacon slice and broiled.

STUFFED HAM

Ham slices stuffed with a mixture of cream cheese, horseradish, chopped green onion and dill.

GOOSE LIVER PATE WITH CHEESE

Prepared goose liver pate with an accompanying group of special cheeses and Loganberry jelly.

To add to the festivities, you may also wish to include the world's best Old Fashioned. Born in Chicago, this dreamy concoction should only be taken with a certain amount of food, for like the Julip, it is potent.
I have a favorite cousin, Linda Casper, who saw *Round Table* race in Chicago with me in 1959, therefore it seems fitting that HER recipe be named after that special occasion.

LINDA'S RACETRACK OLD FASHIONEDS

1½ ounce good, blended whiskey (Jim Bean is a good choice)
½ ounce orange curaco
½ teaspoon fine sugar or 4-5 drops artificial sweetener
Bitters to taste
Club soda
Pineapple cubes, cherries and orange slices for garnish

For each drink, mix 1½ ounce whiskey, ½ ounce curaco, ½ teaspoon sugar, bitters to taste. Stir well until sugar dissolves. Fill glass with club soda and garnish with your choice of pineapple cube, orange slice, or cherries.

After the main event, when the glow of the moment is still warm, and the excitement has slightly abated, the following is my traditional main event dinner for Belmont Eve, as it has become known in our household:

MARINATED TRIPLE CROWN STEAKS

New York steaks, of course!
Worcestershire sauce
Teriyaki sauce
Soy sauce
Catalina dressing
Peanut oil
Dash ginger
Lots of frseh ground pepper

Marinate steaks overnight for best flavor. Depending upon the number of steaks, combine relative amounts of the above ingredients. You may, of course, cook steaks any way you choose, but they are particularly good barbecued.

What better to go with a good steak than a super salad. And what salad could possibly be better than Caesar. Better still, an EASY Caesar.

EASY CAESAR

2 egg yolks
1 tin anchovies
½ cup salad oil
¼ cup Worcestershire
2-4 cloves garlic, to taste
½ teaspoon dry mustard
¼ teaspoon freshly ground pepper
Freshly grated Parmesan cheese

In blender, combine egg yolks, anchovies, oil, Worcestershire sauce, garlic, mustard and pepper. Blend well and refrigerate. Bring to room temperature before using and add Parmesan cheese. Wash Romaine lettuce, toss with dressing until leaves are completely covered and you'll have the best and easiest Caesar imaginable.

Another good dish to serve with your super steaks and tangy Caesar is "Elegant Green Beans" a dish bequeathed to me by the friend of a friend. They are truly,

JANET'S CAN'T LOSE GREEN BEANS

4 cups canned or fresh green beans, reserve 1 cup liquid
¼ cup chopped onion
3 tablespoons butter
2 tablespoons flour
2 tablespoons sugar
2 tablespoons vinegar
¼ cup fresh parsley
1 cup sour cream
3 slices crisp cooked bacon

Cook onion in butter until soft. Stir in flour. Add bean liquid, sugar, vinegar and parsley; cook until thickened, stirring constantly. Add sour cream, then beans. Heat, but do not boil. Crumble bacon over top.

Even people who don't like vegetables perk up at this one!
If someone wishes to add a baked potato to this feast, there will be no objection from this traditionalist.

How do you top off a super dinner like this? How do you top off a super race like the Belmont?
Well, a bottle of Mouton Cadet is nice with dinner, but nothing but the best will do for dessert.
This recipe was given to me by a very special friend, a horse lover, of course. Like the Caesar salad, it is elegant and simple at the same time:

JERRY'S MY DEBUTANTE CHOCOLATE MOUSSE

1 6-ounce package semi-sweet chocolate pieces
2 tablespoons Kahlua
2 eggs
2 egg yolks
1 teaspoon vanilla
¼ cup sugar
1 tablespoon orange juice
1 cup whipping cream
Whipped cream and shaved chocolate for garnish

Melt chocolate with Kahlua in a double boiler over low heat. Meanwhile, put in the blender: eggs, egg yolks, vanilla, sugar and orange juice. Add melted chocolate and blend. Add whipping cream and blend again. Pour into dessert glasses and chill thoroughly. Garnish with whipped cream and shaved chocolate.

Now that the Triple Crown is over for another year and you're ready to begin your diet, I could suggest still a few more things, but dieting is no fun. So we'll leave you with a Marlboro Cup Cheeseburger — largely a tribute to my wonderful uncle, Dick, who knew more about the kitchen than I did!

THE MARLBORO BURGER

1 pound ground beef
½ cup chopped green onions
½ cup chopped green bell pepper
¼ cup steak sauce
1½ teaspoon dry mustard
Salt and pepper to taste
4 slices Cheddar cheese
4 slices Monterey Jack cheese
4 hamburger buns

To ground beef, add onions, pepper, steak sauce, mustard and salt and pepper to taste. Grill and place under broiler to melt cheeses placed on top. Serve on heated, grilled buns.
Happy Triple Crown to all, and to all a good meal.

BIOGRAPHY — ELLEN PARKER

Ellen Parker, wife of Turf & Sports Digest and Horseman's Journal columnist Ron Parker was born 38 years ago in Ohio.

Ellen's interest began in the late 1950's with the advent of the major stakes winner and champion *Round Table.* She visits the old warrior whenever possible from her home in Oakland, California and during her last visit helped the 1958 Horse of the Year celebrate his 30th birthday with a cake.

Ellen has held a number of jobs in racing working for, among others the Jockey Club Statistical Bureau in Lexington, as News Editor at Golden Gate Fields in Albany, California and later as Managing Editor of The Northern California Thoroughbred, based in Santa Rosa, California. Her current status of free-lance turf writer became permanent in 1982 when she married her columnist husband and moved south from Santa Rosa.

From that time, Ellen has had articles published in The Horseman's Journal, The Thoroughbred Record, The Thoroughbred of California, The California Horseman, The Backstretch, The Texas Thoroughbred and Turf and Sport Digest. Ellen authors a regular column for Turf & Sport and is the regular Northern California correspondent for The Thoroughbred of California.

Working with her husband is one of her greatest joys and when it is possible to collaborate on an article, she is proudest to see their names in print together. Her hobbies: horses, horses and more horses. But she occasionally finds time to cook, as "Triple Crown Winners" indicates.

Index

Recipe Index

Contributor Index

RECIPE INDEX

A

RECIPE INDEX

C

D

E

F

G

H

I

J

N

O

P

R

S

Y

Z

CONTRIBUTOR INDEX

A

B

C

I am submitting my favorite recipes to *PROVEN PERFORMANCES II.*
NAME OF RECIPE (Use your name or a racing term; be creative)

_____

CATEGORY _____
LIST OF INGREDIENTS (List in order of use, give precise measurements)

_____
_____
_____
_____
_____

PREPARATION (Include length of cooking time, oven temperature, or degree of heat on top of stove, microwave instructions if applicable)

_____
_____
_____
_____
_____
_____
_____
_____
_____

NUMBER OF SERVINGS _____
ORIGIN OF RECIPE (If Known) _____
HELPFUL HINTS OR COMMENTS_____
Be sure to send more than one recipe. Some recipes may be adapted or discarded because of duplication.
I HAVE GIVEN *PROVEN PERFORMANCES* PERMISSION TO USE MY RECIPE.

_____
(SIGN)
CAREER HIGHLIGHTS OR RACING INTERESTS _____

_____
_____

NAMES AND ADDRESS OF GREAT COOKS IN THE RACING INDUSTRY THAT SHOULD BE CONTACTED: _____

_____
_____

SEND TO: Bobbee Ferrer
          3321 Ridgeway Drive
          Metairie, Louisiana 70002

PROVEN PERFORMANCES
3321 Ridgeway Drive
Metairie, Louisiana 70002

Please send_____copies of PROVEN PERFORMANCES at $13.50 plus $1.50 for postage and handling. Louisiana residents add 94¢ for (7%) sales tax. Enclosed is my check or money order for $_____.

Name _____

Address _____

City _____ State_____ Zip_____

PROVEN PERFORMANCES
3321 Ridgeway Drive
Metairie, Louisiana 70002

Please send_____copies of PROVEN PERFORMANCES at $13.50 plus $1.50 for postage and handling. Louisiana residents add 94¢ for (7%) sales tax. Enclosed is my check or money order for $_____.

Name _____

Address _____

City _____ State_____ Zip_____

PROVEN PERFORMANCES
3321 Ridgeway Drive
Metairie, Louisiana 70002

Please send_____copies of PROVEN PERFORMANCES at $13.50 plus $1.50 for postage and handling. Louisiana residents add 94¢ for (7%) sales tax. Enclosed is my check or money order for $_____.

Name _____

Address _____

City _____ State_____ Zip_____
